THE FOCAL EASY

ADOBE®
ENCORE™
DVD 2.0

The Focal Easy Guide Series

Focal Easy Guides are the best choice to get you started with new software, whatever your level. Refreshingly simple, they do not attempt to cover everything, focusing solely on the essentials needed to get immediate results.

Ideal if you need to learn a new software package quickly, the Focal Easy Guides offer an effective, time-saving introduction to the key tools, not hundreds of pages of confusing reference material. The emphasis is on quickly getting to grips with the software in a practical and accessible way to achieve professional results.

Highly, illustrated in color, explanations are short and to the point. Written by professionals in a user-friendly style, the guides assume some computer knowledge and an understanding of the general concepts in the area covered, ensuring they aren't patronizing!

Series editor: Rick Young (www.digitalproduction.net)

Director and Founding Member of the UK Final Cut User Group, Apple Solutions Expert and freelance television director/editor, Rick has worked for the BBC, Sky, ITN, CNBC and Reuters. Also a Final Cut Pro Consultant and author of the best-selling *The Easy Guide to Final Cut Pro*.

Titles in the series:

The Easy Guide to Final Cut Pro 3, Rick Young
The Focal Easy Guide to Final Cut Pro 4, Rick Young
The Focal Easy Guide to Final Cut Pro 5, Rick Young
The Focal Easy Guide to Final Cut Express, Rick Young
The Focal Easy Guide to DVD Studio Pro 3, Rick Young
The Focal Easy Guide to Maya 5, Jason Patnode
The Focal Easy Guide to Discreet Combustion 3, Gary M. Davis
The Focal Easy Guide to Combustion 4, Gary M. Davis
The Focal Easy Guide to Premiere Pro, Tim Kolb
The Focal Easy Guide to Adobe Premiere Pro 2.0, Tim Kolb
The Focal Easy Guide to Flash MX 2004, Birgitta Hosea
The Focal Easy Guide to Flash Macromedia Flash 8, Birgitta Hosea
The Focal Easy Guide to Cakewalk Sonar, Trev Wilkins
The Focal Easy Guide to Photoshop CS2, Brad Hinkel
The Focal Easy Guide to After Effects, Curtis Sponsler
The Focal Easy Guide to Adobe Encore DVD 2.0, Jeff Bellune

THE FOCAL EASY GUIDE TO

ADOBE® ENCORE™ DVD 2.0

JEFF BELLUNE

AMSTERDAM • BOSTON • HEIDELBERG • LONDON • OXFORD
NEW YORK • PARIS • SAN DIEGO • SAN FRANCISCO
SINGAPORE • SYDNEY • TOKYO

Focal Press is an imprint of Elsevier

Acquisitions Editor: Christine Tridente/Becky Golden-Harrell
Project Manager: Brandy Lilly
Assistant Editor: Robin Weston
Marketing Manager: Christine Degon Veroulis
Cover Design: Fred Rose

Focal Press is an imprint of Elsevier
30 Corporate Drive, Suite 400, Burlington, MA 01803, USA
Linacre House, Jordan Hill, Oxford OX2 8DP, UK

Library of Congress Cataloging in Publication Data
Bellune, Jeff.
   The Focal easy guide to Adobe Encore DVD 2.0/by Jeff Bellune.– 1st ed.
   p.cm.
   Includes bibliographical references and index.
   ISBN-13: 978-0-240-52004-9 (pbk.: alk. paper)
   ISBN-10: 0-240-52004-1 (pbk.: alk. paper)
1.   DVDs.   2.   Interactive multimedia–Authoring programs.
3.   Adobe Encore DVD (Computer file)   I.   Title.
   TK7882.D93B45 2006
   006.6'96–dc22   2006003220

British Library Cataloguing in Publication Data
A catalogue record for this book is available from the British Library.

ISBN 13: 978-0-240-52004-9
ISBN 10: 0-240-52004-1

For information on all Focal Press publications visit
our website at www.books.elsevier.com

05 06 07 08 09 10   10 9 8 7 6 5 4 3 2 1

Working together to grow
libraries in developing countries
www.elsevier.com | www.bookaid.org | www.sabre.org

ELSEVIER   BOOK AID International   Sabre Foundation

Typeset by Charon Tec Ltd, Chennai, India
www.charontec.com
Printed in Italy

For Ann, Ryan, Alex, Avri, Grayson and Garrett; their patient love and support made this book possible. I am proud to be husband and father.

Contents

Introduction   xiii

First Look   1
Hardware   2

Loading the Program   3

Preferences Setup   5
Launching Encore for the First Time   6

General   8

Menus   10

Timelines   11

Preview   12

Encoding   13

Audio/Video Out   14

The Interface   17
Frames and Panels   18

Viewers   19

Workspaces   19

Arranging Workspaces   22

Creating Custom Workspaces   32

Keyboard Shortcuts   33

The Toolbar   34

The Project Panel   35

The Menus Panel   35

The Timelines Panel   35

The Disc Panel   37

The Monitor Panel   38

The Flowchart Panel   38

The Menu Viewer   38

The Properties Panel   40

The Character Panel   40

The Timeline Viewer   40

The Slideshow Viewer   41

The Library Panel   41

The Styles Panel   42

The Layers Panel   43

The Adobe Help Center   43

The Project: Planning   45

Listing Assets   46

Using a Flowchart   46

Workflow   48

The Project: Importing Assets   51

Rules for Imported Assets   52

Importing Assets   55

The Import as Asset Command   55

The Import as Timeline Command   56

The Import as Slideshow Command   57

The Import as Menu Command   60

A Second Look at the Project Panel   61

Locating and Replacing Assets   62

The Project: Transcoding   65

Transcode Settings   68

Transcoding Assets Within Encore   72

Transcoding Assets Before Import   73

The Project: Timeline Creation 75

The Timeline Editing Workspace 76

Creating a Timeline 76

The Timeline Viewer 78

Navigating in the Timeline Viewer 78

The Monitor Panel 80

Adding Chapter Markers 82

Setting a Poster Frame 83

Transcoded Assets and Chapter Markers 85

Navigation Using Chapter Markers 86

Adding Audio Tracks 86

Adding Subtitles 87

Changing the Appearance of Subtitle Text 91

Joining Assets in a Single Timeline 94

The Slideshow Design Workspace 95

Adding Still Images and Audio to a Slideshow 96

The Slideshow Viewer 97

Scaling Slideshow Images 97

Widescreen Slideshows 98

Creating Your Slideshow 99

Arranging the Slides 100

Adding Effects and Transitions to the Slideshow 101

Adding Subtitles to the Slideshow 102

The Project: Menu Design and Creation 105

Encore Menus As Photoshop Files 106

The Menu Design Workspace 107

Getting Started 107

Manipulating Menu Objects 111

The Safe Area 113

Replacing Text in Menu Objects   114

Duplicating Menus and Menu Objects   115

Converting a Text Object to a Button   118

The Subpicture Highlight   120

The Menu Color Set   123

Changing the Appearance of Subpicture Highlights   127

A Special Effect Using Subpicture Highlights   128

Aligning and Distributing Menu Objects   130

Align   131

Distribute   133

Button Routing   135

Building Your Own Menu   138

Static Menu Backgrounds   139

Creating Menus from Backgrounds   140

Using the Library   140

Creating Menu Buttons   142

Creating an Entire Menu External to Encore   143

Adding a Text Object to a Menu   144

The Character Panel   146

Resizing Text Objects   148

Adding Style Effects   149

Adding Background Audio to a Menu   150

Adding Background Video to a Menu   153

Saving Your Work for Use in Future Projects   155

The Project: Linking Everything Together   157

The Navigation Design Workspace   159

First Play   161

End Actions   162

Auto Layout   165

Menu Buttons   166

Sync Button Text and Name   168

Video Thumbnail Buttons   170

Remote Buttons   173

Playlists   174

Chapter Marker End Actions   178

Overrides   180

Setting Allowable User Operations   180

Flowchart Panel Overview   182

Advanced Design Techniques   182

Highlight-Only Menu Buttons   183

Easter Eggs   185

Button Rollover Menus   186

Trivia Quiz Games   188

The Project: Building the DVD   193

Verify Project Settings   194

Checking the Project   195

Correcting Errors   197

Previewing the Project   200

Building a DVD Disc   203

Dual-Layer Discs   204

Building a DVD Folder   206

Building a DVD Image   208

Building a DVD Master   209

Adding DVD-ROM Content   211

Interacting With Other Adobe Software   213

The Edit Original Command   214

Working with Adobe Photoshop   214

The Edit Menu in Photoshop Command   216

Creating Menus in Photoshop   217

Additional Subpicture Highlight Colors   218

Video Placeholder Layers   221

Saving Your Menu   223

Working with Adobe After Effects   225

Animating an Encore Menu in After Effects   227

Working with Adobe Premiere Pro   229

Placing Chapter Markers for Encore   229

Working with Adobe Audition   232

Adobe Bridge   234

Additional Encore DVD Resources   235

Index   237

Introduction

Adobe Encore DVD 2.0 is a great program!

That simple premise is the foundation of this book. Encore is intuitive enough to allow DVD creation with a minimum of fuss, at the same time offering powerful features that let you explore the limits of your creativity. No other DVD authoring package that I have used offers this combination of ease of use and creative power.

I have been getting video out of my computer and onto disc since 1999. DVD was a seemingly magical format back then; only high-powered Hollywood studios (with even higher-powered systems and budgets) could afford to create them. Professional DVD mastering facilities were ridiculously expensive. DVD burners that you could install into your own computer were priced in the thousands of dollars, and the software needed to create those DVDs cost thousands more.

Small business and home enthusiast disc authors were therefore likely to use alternative video formats that could be burned onto CD. CD burners and blank discs were widely available and relatively inexpensive. The biggest disadvantage of these formats was quality. Despite the author's best efforts, oftentimes the quality of the finished disc paled in comparison to what Hollywood was showing could be done with DVD.

Fortunately, advancing technology has made professional DVD authoring available to a wide range of people. What used to be the domain solely of big movie studios is here for you, now. These are exciting times in video editing and production! High-quality DVD presentations that reflect the artistic vision of DVD authors are feasible using tools that take up no more than a desktop's worth of space and whose cost is well within reach.

If you are an experienced DVD author looking to expand your creative horizons, this book will get you up and running with Adobe Encore DVD quickly. You'll also find ways to use Encore to add a big "WOW" factor to your DVDs. Custom menus, including video buttons, background audio, background video and menu transitions can be created easily using Adobe Encore DVD in concert with the other applications in the Adobe Production Studio, or by using your favorite video-editing and graphics programs. Dynamic program content controls and extensive customization tools within Encore allow you to deliver professional-quality discs to your audience and clients that will have them cheering your efforts and returning to you for future projects.

If you are new to DVD authoring, this book will quickly introduce you to some of the concepts behind the technology, and provide a clear roadmap for getting your video out of the computer and onto disc using Adobe Encore DVD. The first time I opened Adobe Encore DVD on my computer, I felt somewhat lost amid the many open, empty windows and the lack of a large button that said, "Start Here". Just as I did, however, you'll soon see that you don't need to be intimidated by Encore's extensive set of tools and customizing capabilities. Adobe Encore DVD is very user-friendly and intuitive. You will be pleasantly surprised at just how quickly and easily you can go from start to finish as you create your DVD. In essence, this book is your "Start Here" button!

I have worked my way through the nooks and crannies of this program and talked with dozens of Adobe Encore DVD users. As you read through the book, you will find that I have anticipated and remember many of the concerns that new authors and new users may have with DVD authoring in general and Encore specifically. When you begin your adventure with Adobe Encore DVD, just remember two things. One, Encore is a great program! That means any issues you face will most likely not be with whether or not Encore can do something, but rather with how Encore does it. Two, use this book. It is your "Easy Guide" to getting your DVD successfully completed!

Let's get started.

First Look

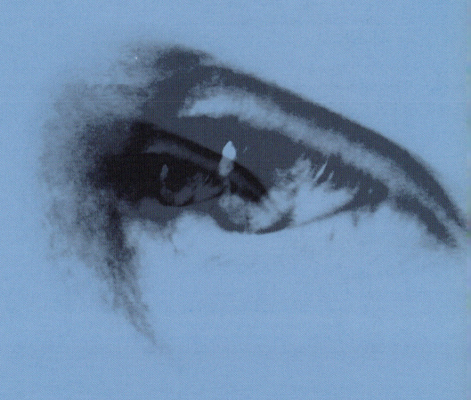

Hardware

To use Adobe Encore DVD 2.0, you will need:

1   A computer running Microsoft Windows XP, updated to Service Pack 2 or higher.

2   An Intel Pentium 4 processor running at 1.4 GHz or faster.

3   512 MB or more of RAM.

4   1 GB of available hard drive space for basic installation and an additional 5 GB of hard disk space for installation of extra content.

5   1280×1024 or greater color monitor resolution and a 32-bit display adapter.

6   A DVD-ROM drive for installation. Unlike most other programs that have a CD as an installation disc, Adobe Encore DVD 2.0 installs from a DVD.

The critical item for the processor is an ability to support the SSE2 instruction set, which eliminates all Pentium 3 and earlier processors, and all AMD Athlon XP and earlier processors, regardless of speed.

You should consider a system that exceeds the recommended requirements – it will make your DVD authoring experience much more enjoyable. It's always a good idea to have as much RAM as you can, but particularly so in this case. With all the new integration-related features of Adobe Encore DVD 2.0, you will most likely want to have Adobe After Effects, Adobe Photoshop or both open at the same time as Encore. To comfortably run Encore and these other applications, you should have at least 1 GB of RAM. You will also need plenty of hard disk space while you work in Encore – it is a good idea to have 10 GB or more available for use. How much more? Hard disk space is relatively inexpensive these days, so an extra 40–60 GB is not unreasonable. The extra disk space will also come in handy if you edit any of the source video for your DVD projects. To put things in perspective, here are some example space requirements for digital video (DV) and audio:

1   DV takes up 13 GB per hour of video.

2   Uncompressed, CD-quality digital audio uses 700 MB per hour of audio.

If you want to burn your own DVDs, you will need a DVD recorder. I recommend a newer, name-brand model with the latest firmware update. Buying an older or off-brand burner is not a good idea because of potential compatibility and operability issues.

If you wish to preview your menus on an external monitor like an NTSC or PAL television, then you will need an IEEE 1394 (Firewire) port on your computer. Most new computers come with this port as part of the system. You will also need a digital-to-analog converter to convert the digital firewire signal to an analog signal that the monitor will understand. There are several external devices available on the market that can convert the signal for you, including most DV camcorders. To connect these devices, you will need at least one of the following cables:

1 A six-pin firewire cable. These cables have large connectors at each end.

2 A four-pin firewire cable. These cables have small connectors at each end.

3 A six-pin-to-four-pin firewire cable. These cables have a large connector at one end and a small connector at the other.

Note: Most external devices have a four-pin connector and most desktop computers use six-pin connectors, so a six-pin-to-four-pin cable is required most of the time. Be sure to check the documentation for your hardware setup.

Loading the Program

Insert the Adobe Encore DVD 2.0 DVD into your DVD-ROM drive or your DVD burner. If you have AutoPlay enabled for that drive, then you will automatically be presented with an AutoPlay Screen that has several options. Otherwise, you will have to navigate to your DVD-ROM drive using Windows Explorer and launch the AutoPlay program manually. Once you have access to the AutoPlay screen, choose the option to "Install Adobe Encore DVD 2.0" and follow the prompts.

During the installation process, you will be introduced to Adobe's version of copy protection. It's called Activation, and it ensures that Adobe Encore DVD 2.0 is not casually copied to multiple computers. You can activate by phone or via the Internet. If you don't want to activate your copy of Encore during installation, you

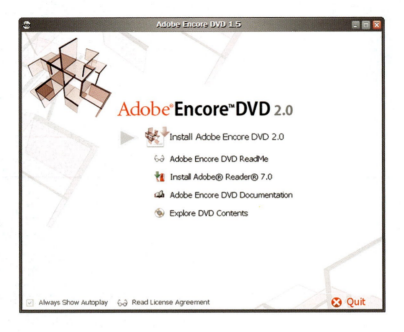

can postpone activation for up to 30 days. However, after the 30-day period is over, Encore will stop working.

If you have any difficulties with the program installation, and especially if you encounter any error messages, be sure to select the "Adobe Encore DVD ReadMe" option on the AutoPlay Screen. It contains terrific troubleshooting information, not just during installation, but for general program use as well. There is a discussion of any known issues with Adobe Encore DVD 2.0. This is an excellent ReadMe document, and if you run into trouble, it can save you lots of time!

Once you have successfully installed Adobe Encore DVD 2.0, you are ready to begin setting up your program preferences.

Preferences Setup

Although many users consider the initial setup of an application to be like having to write an essay on what they did last summer, a quick trip through the Preferences dialog is helpful. The good news is that most of the default preference settings will work very well for almost everything. You should be able to breeze right through this chapter and move on to more enjoyable subjects!

Launching Encore for the First Time

When you launch Encore for the first time, two things will happen that won't occur on subsequent launches. First, the Registration dialog will pop up. By registering your copy of Encore, you gain access to Adobe's technical support and many valuable resources on the Adobe web site. Second, the Library content has to be initialized. It will seem like Encore is taking forever to open, and you may be concerned that the program has stopped responding. Don't worry. It is not unusual for Encore to take 10 minutes or more to initialize the Library.

Each time that you launch Encore, you will be asked to choose between starting a new project and opening an existing project. After you have been working with Encore a while, you will also see a list of recently opened projects.

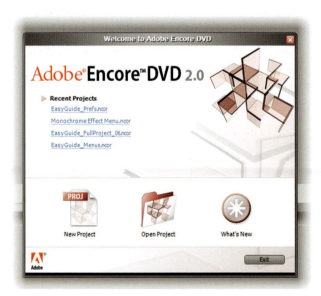

The first time you choose New Project, you will also be prompted for the Television Standard to be used in the project. The choices are NTSC and PAL. Once you choose a standard, it becomes the default for all new projects. You can also choose to tell Encore not to prompt you anymore when you start a new project.

The New Project Settings dialog

Either way, once Encore knows which TV standard to use, you will see a box telling you that Encore is preparing the transcode settings. *Transcoding* is how Encore ensures that all of your assets conform to the worldwide DVD standard before your project is burned to DVD. We will discuss transcode settings in "The Project: Transcoding".

When the main application window opens, you will see several vacant areas under different tabs. Don't worry about that just yet; we'll discuss how to fill those up with useful project stuff in other chapters. For now, select Edit ▶ Preferences ▶ General from the program's Menu Bar.

Preferences ▶ General

User Interface

Adobe Encore DVD 2.0 lets you choose the brightness of the User Interface. The default setting is easy on the eyes, but you may prefer to work with an overall darker or lighter interface.

Checking or unchecking the items under Separate Viewers changes how multiple open viewers for each of the listed viewer types will be arranged. We'll see how this works in "The Interface" chapter.

The "Show tool tips" and "Beep when done" checkboxes are checked by default to provide visual and audio cues that can assist you while you work. If you ever decide you don't want those cues anymore, return here and uncheck them.

Library Content

During installation, the Library was stored in its default location: "C:\Program Files\Adobe\Adobe Encore DVD 2.0\Library". If space becomes limited on your Windows drive, you can move the entire Library folder to another hard disk. After you have moved the Library, use the Library Content setting to point Encore to the new location of the Library. Moving the Library will free up some room on your Windows drive and make more space available for additional Library items that you might add in the future. Library Content that you add will always be stored in your personal Windows XP folders, located under "C:\Documents and Settings". You cannot change the location where Encore stores added Library Content.

Be aware that when you move the Library, the content has to be re-initialized. It will again take several minutes for Encore to initialize the Library. When you close the Preferences dialog by clicking OK, Encore will immediately begin initializing the Library. That might be a good time to go get a cup of coffee while you wait for the process to finish.

Television Standard for New Projects

This preference tells Encore what the default setting for new projects should be. If you work primarily with NTSC video, then choose NTSC. Otherwise, choose PAL. If you told Encore not to prompt you anymore for the Television Standard when you start a new project, this is the setting that will be used for all of your new projects. If you later need to change the standard for new projects, this is the place to do it.

Playback Quality

This setting determines quality of playback during project Preview and when working in the Monitor panel. "The Project: Timeline Creation" has more information about how each of these settings affects playback. If your system meets or exceeds Adobe's recommended system requirements, then you will probably like the High setting best.

Reset Warning Dialogs

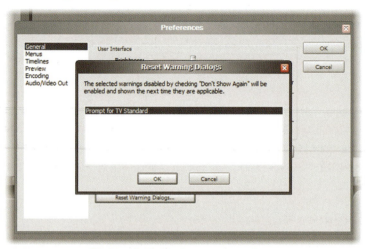

The list of disabled program warnings

Pressing this button brings up a dialog box that lists all of the warnings that you have told Encore not to warn you about anymore. You can select any or all of them to be reset.

Preferences ▶ Menus

This screen is where you specify the default *button routing* for your menus in Encore. Button routing describes which button on a menu will be selected next when the audience pushes one of the directional arrows/navigation keys on the DVD player's remote control. *Wrapping* refers to what should happen when the audience presses a navigation key that would otherwise move the selection off-screen.

When you edit a menu in Encore, you can specify the exact routing you want to have for each button on each menu. The corresponding choices you make in the Menu viewer always override any of the default settings listed here. Consequently, you probably won't need to change these settings from their default.

Preferences ▶ Timelines

When you create a new Timeline, this is where Encore looks to see how many audio and subtitle tracks it should add.

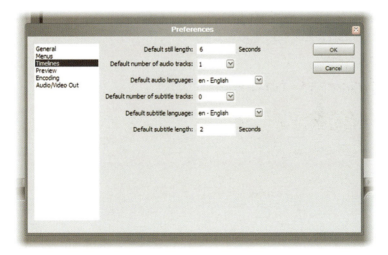

Default Still Length

This setting lets Encore know how long to display a still image on-screen before moving to the next image or video clip. The default still length of 6 seconds applies to still images that are added to Timelines and Slideshows in Encore. This setting is less important for Slideshows than for Timelines because it is very easy to change the slide duration in Slideshows for some or all of the still images in the show.

Default Subtitle Length

This setting tells Encore how long to make each new subtitle when it is added to a Timeline. You can easily change the length of the subtitles after they are in the Timeline. This is another setting that probably will not have to be changed from the default.

Preferences ▶ Preview

The settings listed here only affect the Preview of your project inside of Encore. They have no effect on your project when you build it and burn it to disc.

TV Mode

The default is 4:3 Letter Box, which displays full-frame video as full-frame and widescreen video in a letter box format. If you want to preview widescreen video as it would appear on a widescreen television, choose 16:9. Full-frame video that is previewed using the 16:9 setting will appear stretched and distorted.

Player Region Code

You can simulate the playback of your disc on different DVD players from around the world. Note that you cannot set the region code for the disc itself from this dialog box; this setting is for project preview only.

Audio and Subtitle Language

If you have multiple audio and/or subtitle tracks in your project, then these settings determine which one will be played as the default when you preview your project. Again, these are preview-only settings and do not affect the finished project.

Preferences ▶ Encoding

Audio Encoding Scheme

This setting tells Encore how to encode audio that is used in your projects. I recommend using Dolby Digital all the time because it gives high-quality audio playback and takes up very little space on the finished DVD. The less space that audio takes up on the disc, the more space that is available for video. And that translates directly to higher video quality.

Maximum Automatic Transcoding Bit Rate

Encore uses this setting to determine the maximum allowable bit rate that will be used for encoding video into a format that DVD players will recognize. Because some DVD players have trouble playing recorded discs with high bit rates, I recommend setting this to 7.00 megabits per second, to ensure maximum compatibility with existing DVD players, while at the same time preserving the high quality of the original video.

Preferences ▶ Audio/Video Out

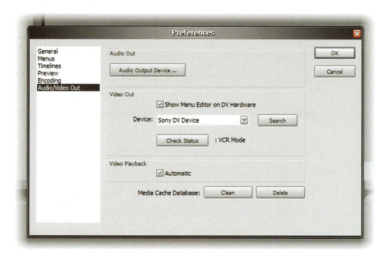

Audio Out

Pressing the Audio Output Device button brings up a list of the audio devices on your computer that Encore recognizes. If you have more than one sound card or audio device installed in your system, here is where you tell Encore which one to use. This setting does not affect the finished disc; it is used for Encore's previews only.

Note: ASIO sound cards that do not have Windows Audio drivers will appear in Encore as stereo-only, even though they are obviously capable of multichannel sound reproduction.

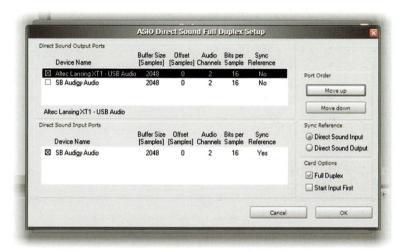

The system's audio devices that can be used by Encore

Video Out

If you have a DV device like a camcorder, digital-to-analog converter or tape deck connected to your system via an IEEE 1394 (Firewire) cable, then checking the Show Menu Editor on DV Hardware checkbox will let you preview the Menu Viewer on that device. Note that Project Preview and Timeline playback are not available via Firewire.

If you have multiple DV devices connected to your computer, then you can select which one you want Encore to use in the Device box.

If you are sure that you have a DV device connected via Firewire to your computer and turned on, but Encore does not list it, you can click on the Search button to force Encore to look again.

If your DV device is listed in the Device box and turned on, but is showing offline, you can force Encore to check its status again by clicking on the Check Status button.

Note: Forcing Encore to check again for devices and their status is usually only necessary if you connect a DV device while Encore is running.

Video Playback

On most computers, Encore can tell what the correct settings are for playing back video. On some systems, Encore can't tell what the settings should be and won't be able to playback video at all. This setting does not address the quality of Video Playback – either there is video or there is not. If there is, then Automatic is the correct setting. Return here and uncheck Automatic to try and troubleshoot a complete lack of video inside of Encore.

Media Cache Database

This database is shared by the audio and video applications in the Adobe Production Studio. The files in the Media Cache are created as you work in these programs so that all the programs can run faster. Clicking on Clean removes any old cached files; clicking Delete discards the database that tracks the files. If you need to free up disk space, use Clean. Delete the database to troubleshoot a project.

Once you are happy with the changes you have made to Encore's Preferences, click OK. If you're unsure about what's been changed, or if you would like to start over, click Cancel.

As you gain more experience working with Encore, you may decide to make changes to the settings that will better suit the way you work inside the program. You can revisit the Preferences dialog at any time.

The Interface

The interface in Adobe Encore DVD 2.0 is brand new and greatly improved over previous versions. It wastes almost no space and rearranging the working area is fast and efficient. Despite its very different feel, you may soon wish that all your programs worked like this!

Since this interface paradigm is new to Encore specifically and to Windows in general, I'm going to take a little bit of extra time to cover how it works.

Frames and Panels

The interface is made up of several *frames* that consist of one or more *panels*.

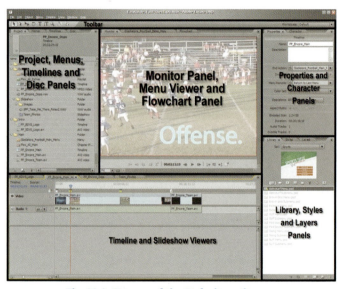

The Main Frames of the Default workspace

Each individual panel is accessed by a tab at the top of the frame. The frames are resizable inside the main application window. Each of these frames used to be a separate window in earlier versions of Encore. By switching to this new frames-and-panel layout, Adobe has converted the space that would have been required for titlebars, status bars, buttons and other window stuff into usable screen real estate.

If you have a dual-monitor computer desktop, the space created by the new interface design is a bonus. But more importantly, this additional space is very good news for DVD authors who use a single-monitor computer desktop, and for authors who are creating projects on laptops while traveling. For the purposes of this book, we will work with layouts optimized for single-monitor systems.

Viewers

Encore has four special panels that are called *viewers*. Viewers are panels that can have more than one instance of the panel open at one time. The four viewers are:

1 Chapter Playlist viewer.

2 Menu viewer.

3 Slideshow viewer.

4 Timeline viewer.

You can choose to have multiple viewers organized under one tab with a drop-down list, or organized using separate tabs for each instance of the viewer. You can even choose to have different organization strategies for each viewer.

Often you can work more efficiently with multiple viewers if each tab is available separately for single-click access. Conversely, having all viewer instances organized under a single tab with a drop-down list can help maintain a clean, uncluttered workspace; important when screen real estate is at a premium. Change your preference for how each of the viewer types is displayed by checking or unchecking the choice for separate viewers under Edit ▶ Preferences ▶ General.

Workspaces

Adobe Encore DVD 2.0 ships with several pre-designed workspaces. Each one is adjusted to make its supported task as efficient as possible. Access them from

THE FOCAL EASY GUIDE TO ADOBE® ENCORE™ DVD 2.0

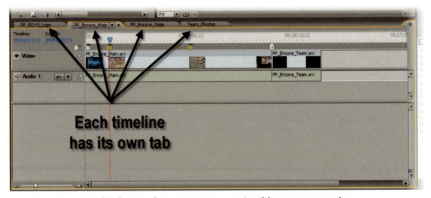

Multiple Timeline viewers organized by separate tabs

Multiple Menu viewers organized under a single tab
using a drop-down list

the Window ▶ Workspace menu item. We'll reference the Default workspace for this discussion, but as we move into other parts of the project, we will explore the other workspace presets in more detail. Here are samples of some of the included workspaces:

20

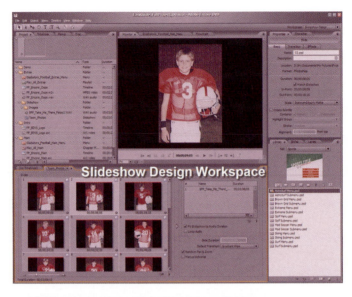

Arranging Workspaces

It is easy to modify workspaces by arranging the tabbed panels to fit the way you work. Rearrangement is accomplished by dragging and dropping the tabs and by accessing the commands available in the *wing menu* of each frame.

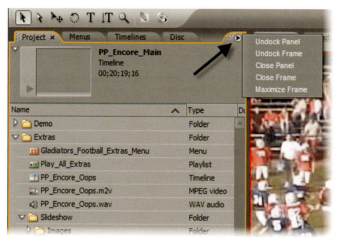

The frame wing menu

Using a frame's wing menu, you can *undock*, or remove, a panel or an entire frame. When you undock a panel or a frame, it automatically becomes a floating window that hovers above the other frames.

One particularly useful command available on the wing menu is the Maximize Frame command. It does exactly what you would expect it to do. Using this command from a frame's wing menu fills the entire workspace with the frame.

Once a frame is maximized, a new command becomes available on the wing menu for that frame: the Restore Frame Size command. Using this command puts everything in the workspace back to where it was before you maximized the frame.

To quickly toggle between a maximized frame and a restored workspace, use the keyboard shortcut (~). When you edit and design menus for your DVD, and when you use the new Flowchart tab, you will really appreciate the ability to switch quickly between these two layouts.

For drag-and-drop rearranging, or *docking*, Encore provides strong visual cues, called *drop zones*, which show you exactly where a panel will land when the mouse button is released. There are two different colors used for the drop zones: purple and green.

A floating window. Notice how It hovers over the other frames

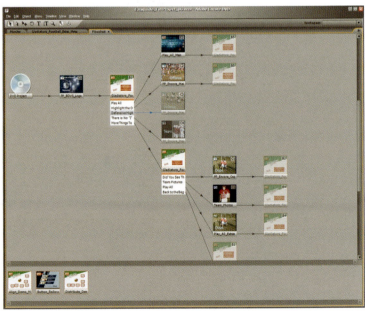

The Flowchart panel's frame is maximized

To dock panels using drag-and-drop:

1 Click on the tab for the panel that you want to move, to bring it to the front of its frame.

2 Position your cursor over the group of dots, called a *gripper*, to left of the text on the tab and begin to drag the tab towards the intended target frame.

The tab gripper

3 While you are dragging, take note of which drop zone in the target frame is highlighted:

- Dropping the panel onto the largest purple zone in the center of the target frame will dock it in the frame.
- Dropping the panel onto the smallest purple zone over the tabs at the top of the target frame will also dock it in the frame.

Docking to the center of the frame

- Dropping the panel onto one of the smaller purple zones that appear at the top, bottom and sides of the target frame will create a new frame to that side and dock the panel within it. Space for the new frame will be taken from the target frame and, if necessary, an adjacent frame.

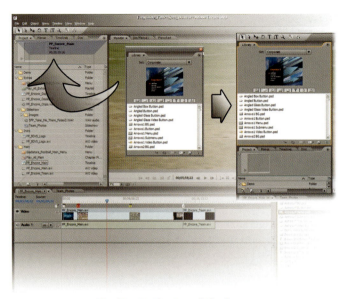

Docking to the top of the frame

Docking to the bottom of the frame

Docking to the left side of the frame

Docking to the right side of the frame

- Dropping the panel onto a green drop zone at the extreme left, right, top or bottom edges of the application window will create a new frame that stretches the entire vertical or horizontal length of the application window and contains the docked panel. Space for the new frame will be taken equally from all the other frames.

4 Dock the panel by releasing the mouse button.

Docking to the edge of the application window

To resize a frame:

1 Position your cursor at the edge or at the corner of the frame.

2 At any of the edges, the cursor changes to a double-lined, double-headed arrow. You can change the size of the frame in the one dimension that is indicated by the arrows.

3 At the corners, the cursor changes to a four-pointed arrow. You can change the size of the frame in two dimensions at the same time.

4 Drag the frame until it is the size you want. Each frame has a minimum recommended size that changes based on what panels are included in the frame. As you drag to resize the frame, the frame edges will snap to this minimum size. You can override Encore's minimum size recommendation by continuing to drag past the snapping point.

The cursor icons used for resizing frames

If a frame does not have enough space to show the tabs of all the panels that are docked there, a small slider will appear just above the tabs in that frame.

To reorder the tabs in a frame:

1 Position your cursor over the gripper for the tab you want to move.

2 Drag the tab left or right. The tab display for the frame will show the updated tab order before you release the mouse button. If you see a drop zone highlighted in the frame, then you have moved the tab up or down as well as left or right. Move your cursor back into the tab row and restrict your mouse movement to left or right only.

3 When you see the tabs in the order you want, drop the tab.

Use the slider to scroll to a Tab that is hidden

To undock a panel using drag-and-drop:

1 As you drag the tab for the panel, hold down the Ctrl key.

2 Drop the panel anywhere, while still pressing the Ctrl key. A new window will be created that contains the panel. This window will hover on top of the other frames.

To close a panel, do any one of the following:

1 Click the small "x" to the right of the text in panel's tab.

2 Open the wing menu for the frame that contains the panel and choose Close Panel.

To close a frame, do any one of the following:

1 Open the frame's wing menu and choose Close Frame.

2 Close all the panels in the frame one-by-one.

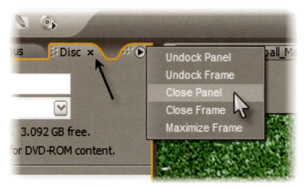

Options for closing a panel

To close one or more instances of a viewer:

1   Click the drop-down arrow to the right of the name text in the viewer's tab.

2   Select Close to close the current instance of the viewer.

3   Select Close All to close all viewer instances but leave a blank viewer open as a placeholder in the frame.

The Close and Close All options for a viewer

Note: As long as at least one frame is open, Encore won't let you leave any empty space inside the application window. If you move all of the panels out of a frame, or close all of a frame's panels, the remaining frames will expand as necessary to fill the space.

To open a closed panel or viewer:

1   For any panel or viewer: go to the Window menu and choose the panel or viewer you want to open. It will open in the appropriate frame, even if that frame had been closed previously.

2 For viewers only: double-click the element in the Project panel that corresponds to the viewer you want to open. It will open in the appropriate frame.

Play with rearranging and resizing panels and frames until you get a feel for how this powerful new feature works. If you get to the point where you think that you have created an awful mess out of the workspace, don't worry. Select the Window ▶ Workspace ▶ Reset Workspace menu command and Encore will put everything back just the way it was before you started redecorating.

Creating Custom Workspaces

Encore lets you modify existing workspaces in two ways: workspaces can be *updated* or *saved*. The current workspace is updated automatically as you make changes to the layout. If, for example, you start with the Default pre-designed workspace and decide to make the Timeline viewer a little shorter and a bit wider, then the Default workspace will be updated with the new Timeline viewer size. The next time you select the Default workspace, it will open with the new layout.

Note: Updates to the current workspace cannot be undone using the Undo command. You must use the Window ▶ Workspace ▶ Reset Workspace command to undo workspace updates.

After a workspace has been updated by layout changes, it can then be saved – either as a new workspace or as a permanent change to the current workspace.

To save the current layout as a new workspace:

1 Go to the Window ▶ Workspace menu.

2 Select New Workspace.

3 Give your workspace a new name and click OK.

To permanently change the current workspace and save it with the modified layout:

1 Go to the Window ▶ Workspace menu.

2 Select New Workspace.

3   Enter the name of the current workspace and click OK.

4   When Encore asks you if you would like to replace the workspace,
click Yes.

If you reset any future updates to the saved workspace, the layout will return to
the saved configuration.

Note: If you use this method to replace any of the pre-designed workspaces
that shipped with Adobe Encore DVD 2.0, then the original, pre-designed
configuration will be lost.

Keyboard Shortcuts

Throughout this book I will reference keyboard shortcuts for mouse operations that
can speed up your workflow. Keyboard shortcuts will be enclosed in parentheses;
for example, if you should hold down the Ctrl key while you press the F4 key, the
keyboard shortcut will be shown as (Ctrl+F4).

The Toolbar

In the Default workspace, the toolbar stretches across the top of the application window. On the left side are the available tools and on the right side is a drop-down list from which you can change workspaces.

Note: The drop-down list will be blank when you open a previously saved project. That allows you to make changes to the layout without affecting existing workspaces. If you subsequently select a workspace from the Window ▶ Workspace menu or from the toolbar's drop-down list, remember that any future layout changes will update the selected workspace.

The toolbar can be moved like any other tabbed panel by clicking on the gripper for the bar and dragging.

To temporarily hide the toolbar and create some extra space for the other frames, select Window ▶ Tools or use the keyboard shortcut (Ctrl+F4). Repeat to toggle it back into view.

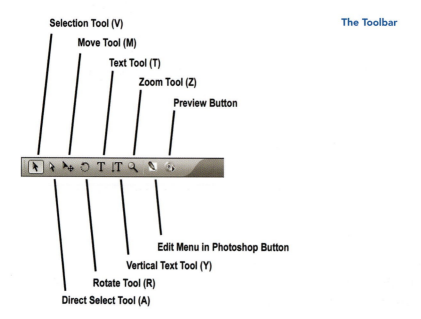

Selection Tool (V)
Move Tool (M)
Text Tool (T)
Zoom Tool (Z)
Preview Button

The Toolbar

Edit Menu in Photoshop Button
Vertical Text Tool (Y)
Rotate Tool (R)
Direct Select Tool (A)

The Project Panel

This panel provides an overview of all the elements in your project. All the video clips, pictures and audio clips that you import into your project are listed here, as well as the timelines, menus, playlists and slideshows that you create.

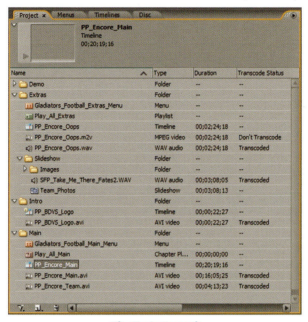

The Project panel

The Menus Panel

The top pane of the Menus panel is a list of all the menus in the project. The bottom pane is a list of all the buttons on the selected menus in the top pane.

The Timelines Panel

Similar to the Menus panel, the top pane of the Timelines panel is a list of all the timelines in the project. The bottom pane is a list of all the chapters in the selected timelines in the top pane.

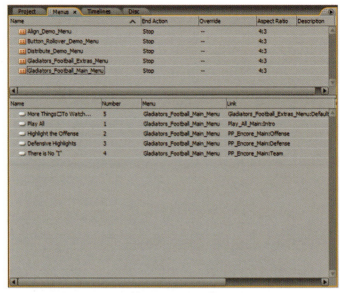

The Menus panel

The Timelines panel

The Disc Panel

The Disc panel summarizes how all the elements in the project will affect the finished disc. It also gives you access to special project and disc operations.

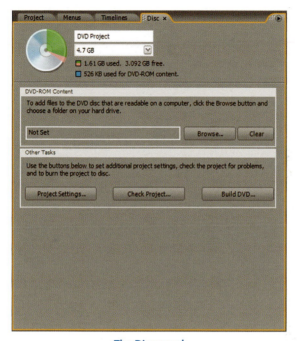

The Disc panel

Use the Disc panel to:

1   See a graphical representation of the disc space used by the project so far.

2   Change the total disc space available for the project.

3   Add DVD-ROM content to the disc.

4   Change project settings like region codes and copy protection.

5   Check the project for errors.

6   Build the project.

The Monitor Panel

The Monitor panel is the playback display for both the Timeline viewer and the Slideshow viewer.

The Monitor panel

The Flowchart Panel

A flowchart of the entire project is displayed in this panel. The top pane shows the elements in the project that have been linked to the root disc. The bottom pane shows *orphan* elements – elements that are not linked to the root disc.

As with the Properties panel, this panel can be used to create and refine links between elements in the project.

The Menu Viewer

The Menu viewer is one of the four special panels that can have more than one instance of itself open at a time. Each time you open a menu from the project window, a new viewer instance is created. You can easily switch between menus by choosing the tab for the menu you want to edit.

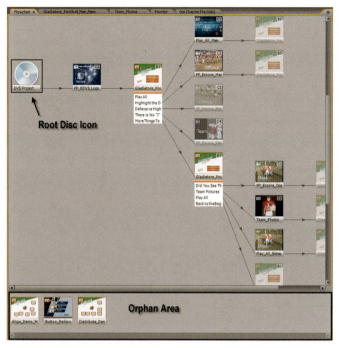

The Flowchart panel showing the Root Disc and the Orphan Area

The Menu viewer showing the tab drop-down list of open menus

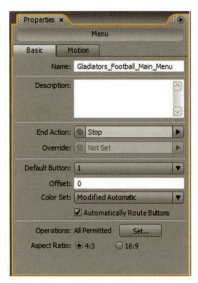

The Properties panel for a menu

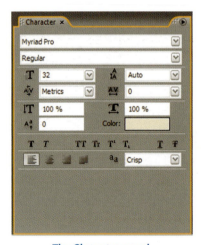

The Character panel

The Properties Panel

When you select an element that is part of the project from any of several panels, the Properties panel displays important information about the selected element. Different information is displayed for different types of elements. However, the Properties panel is not limited to the display of this information; many element properties can be modified from here. You will visit this panel often as you construct your project.

The Character Panel

Here you can manipulate the properties of the text that is used for your menus, buttons and subtitles. If you are used to working with the other applications in the Adobe Production Studio, this panel will be very familiar to you.

The Timeline Viewer

The Timeline viewer is another of the special panels that can have more than one instance of itself open at a time. You can have a Timeline viewer open for one, some or all of the timelines in the project at the same time. The name of the current timeline is displayed in the viewer's tab.

The Timeline viewer shows you the video, audio and subtitle tracks that make up the current timeline.

The timeline viewer showing one video, one audio and one subtitle track

The Slideshow Viewer

As with the Timeline and Menu viewers, you can have one or more Slideshow viewers open at the same time. The current slideshow is displayed in the viewer, and you can quickly see other slideshows by selecting the tab for the slideshow you want.

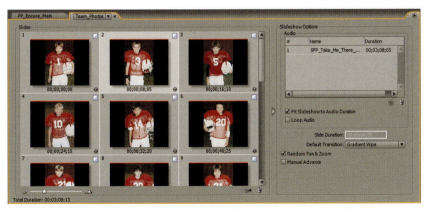

The Slideshow viewer showing the selected picture with information about the picture and the slideshow

The Library Panel

The Library panel provides access to the menus and menu objects that are part of the Encore Library. From here you can create new menus and add objects to existing menus in your project. You can use the Library to store graphic and text objects from your projects, or even complete menus, that you want to use again in other projects. The objects in the Library are organized by category, or *Set*, and by type – Menu, Button, Background, etc.

The Library panel showing just the menus and buttons in the corporate set. The default menu in the set is highlighted

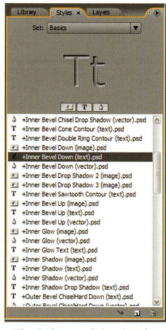

The Styles panel showing the inner bevel down style as it would be applied to text

The Styles Panel

A *style* combines several individual effects like drop shadows and bevels to create more complex effects – metallic or glass shapes, for example. The Styles panel contains pre-defined styles that can be applied to text and to graphic objects. Like the Library panel, the styles are organized by set and type. Using these styles on simple graphics and text can save you a lot of design time compared to the time it would take to recreate these effects yourself in a graphics program.

The Layers Panel

The Layers panel shows all the layers that make up the menu that is currently displayed in the Menu viewer. Don't fret if you don't know what a layer is or why there's a plus sign in front of some layer names. We'll get into the Layers panel in much more detail in "The Project: Menu Design and Creation".

The Layers panel showing all the layers of the menu that is currently displayed in the Menu viewer

The Adobe Help Center

The Help system for Encore uses a little mini-application called the Adobe Help Center (AHC) which is a single interface that can load help files for several

Adobe applications. The first time you ask for help inside of Encore, it may take several seconds for the AHC to start and load the Encore files. Be patient. This is normal, and the AHC will load faster on subsequent help requests.

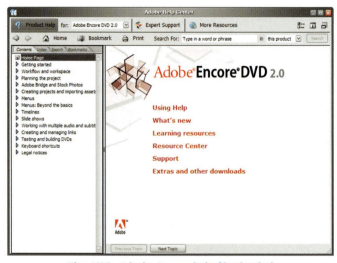

The AHC with the Encore help files loaded

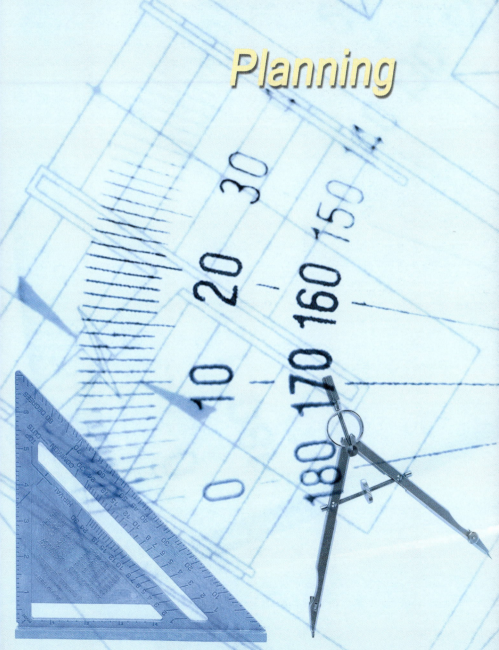

THE PROJECT:

Planning

THE FOCAL EASY GUIDE TO ADOBE® ENCORE™ DVD 2.0

Since you are probably anxious to start creating your DVD, it is understandable if the thought of planning does not generate much enthusiasm. However, the foundation of any successful Encore project is planning. Whether you are creating an independent film for distribution, a family video, an interactive video for a kiosk at a public location or a training video for a corporate client, all DVD projects will benefit from a good plan. Planning your project properly will keep you organized, focused and minimize any frustration with Encore and the DVD creation process. The good news is that your plan doesn't require a team of engineers, a librarian or a relational database. Plans can be as detailed or as cursory as you would like; the essential ingredient is that you have a basic idea of how you want your finished DVD to look and operate.

Listing Assets

A DVD is a collection of video, audio and graphics that are linked together. Each video clip, audio file or graphics file that you bring into Encore is called an *asset*. The process of collecting and linking all these assets together is called *authoring*. To successfully author your DVD in a way that is logical and not confusing, the links between assets need to be mapped out. Simply put, you have to decide how the viewer will get from the menus to the media and back again.

The first step in planning your project is to list the assets that you want to use. Once you have that list, you can begin to map the links that will define how the viewer interacts with your finished DVD.

Using a Flowchart

My favorite planning tool is a flowchart drawn by hand on paper. Now, the word "flowchart" may cause some of you to want to get up and go get a couple of aspirin, but there's no need for that. If you can't remember whether a diamond or a square represents a decision step or if you wonder why circles are needed at all, don't worry. Your flowchart isn't going to be graded. You shouldn't care if the right shapes are in the right place or even what shapes should be used. This tool is for you; for your planning only. You are creating a visual representation of your project that makes sense to you; one where your assets are linked the way you want the project to flow and where no assets are left out. An outline can be useful as well, much like what you would do if you were "authoring" a book. The important thing is to get the organization of your DVD down on paper.

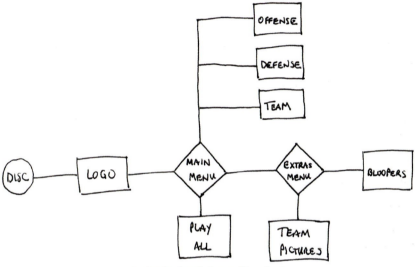

A simple, hand-drawn flowchart

When you first begin mapping the links in the project, you probably won't have the menus completely defined. You may want to visit Encore's library of menus, buttons and backgrounds to get an idea of how you want your menus to look. Even if you have already created the graphics and video assets you will use as backgrounds for the menus and buttons, most likely you will not yet know which links to which assets belong on which menu. This is the most important result of good planning: as you map out the links between assets, the menu structure and program flow for the entire disc will take shape and become clear.

Adobe Encore DVD 2.0 has a great new flowchart feature that lets you quickly establish links to your assets using the same metaphor as a hand-drawn flowchart. And, as the project moves forward, you may find that you need to alter or tweak your plan by adding or removing assets or changing links. The flowchart panel is a very dynamic tool that can help you easily make and track changes to your project. This panel will be discussed in more detail in "The Project: Linking Everything Together".

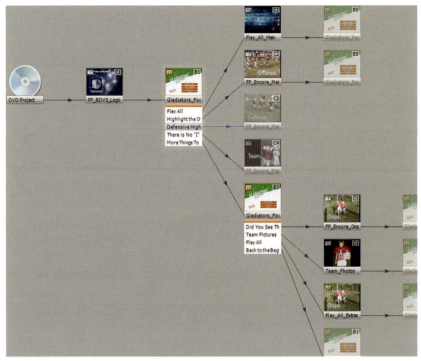

Project represented by Encore's flowchart

Workflow

Once you have a list of your assets and how you want them to be linked together, you are ready to begin your project in earnest. The workflow that is used in this book will help you to see your project through to completion. We will use this workflow to build an example project, with the flowchart shown above as the foundation. Here is a general overview of the steps that are needed to author a DVD with Adobe Encore DVD 2.0:

1   Import your assets into Encore and organize them.

2   Create timelines using imported assets.

3   Create menus using Encore's library or using your own graphics.

4   Link menu buttons to timelines, menu buttons to other menus and timelines to other timelines to create the disc's navigation and special effects.

5   Check the project for errors that could affect the creation and playability of your finished disc.

6   Build the project.

Authoring a DVD is not a strictly linear process. For example, you don't always have to create timelines before you create menus, and you can build parts of your project early on instead of waiting to build the whole thing at the end. The workflow that is outlined above is a tool to get you started while you become familiar with Adobe Encore DVD 2.0. As you become more experienced at authoring DVDs, you will find a workflow that best fits your vision and skill.

As we work our way through the example project, a lot of the how-to steps will be quite general in nature and will apply to any project. However, many of the steps will be tutorial-style and apply specifically to the example project. I chose to set things up this way so that you could see not only the "theory" behind authoring a DVD with Adobe Encore DVD 2.0, but also have practical applications of the theory as examples. The best part is that this book doesn't have a companion CD or DVD that has to be loaded in order for you to follow along; in fact, you don't even have to be at your computer while you read! The illustrations accompanying the text are sufficient to allow you to follow the creation of our example project from start to finish.

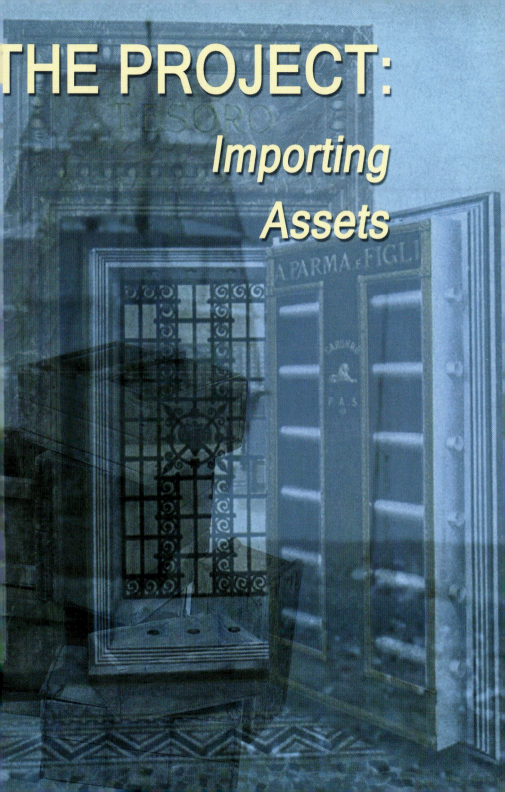

THE PROJECT:

Importing Assets

Now that you know your way around inside of Encore and understand the importance of planning the project, it's time to start filling up some of those blank spaces that you saw when you set up Encore's Preferences. (You did set up your Preferences, didn't you?) Importing assets is a great place to start.

Note: In this chapter you will encounter the terms *timeline, slideshow* and *menu.* Adobe Encore DVD 2.0 offers special import options that allow you to create these project elements at the same time that you import assets. These elements will be discussed in detail in other chapters, so don't worry if you don't see right away how they all fit together in the project.

Rules for Imported Assets

Since Encore is an authoring application that is designed to assemble content instead of to create content, we need to go over the rules about what kind of assets Encore will accept. The rules are broken down here by the type of asset to be imported: video, audio and graphic.

Give this section a quick read, and certainly don't try to memorize all the rules that follow. Instead, use this section as a reference to guide you as you consider how to prepare your assets outside of Encore. You should also check this section again should Encore ever complain about an asset that you are trying to import.

Video Assets

Encore can import video in several different formats. It will accept Windows video (.avi and .wmv), MPEG video (.mpg, .mpeg, .m2v and .mpv) and QuickTime video (.mov), including QuickTime reference files. Encore is very strict about what frame sizes and frame rates can be imported, so you must ensure that you properly prepare your video before you bring it into Encore. Here are the allowable frame sizes (in pixels) and frame rates (in frames per second):

1. NTSC video can have a frame size of 720×480, 720×486 or 704×480. The allowable frame rates for NTSC video are 29.97, 23.976, 23.978 and 24 fps.

2   PAL video is supported at a frame rate of 25 fps and frame sizes of 720×576 and 704×576.

3   NTSC video at other than 29.97 fps (regardless of format) will be transcoded immediately on import to convert it to 29.97 fps.

Whether the screen size, more properly called the *screen aspect ratio*, of the video portions of your finished DVD will be *Standard* or *Widescreen* is determined by the *pixel aspect ratio* (PAR) of your video assets. PAR is the ratio of the width to the height of each pixel in an asset.

1   NTSC DVD video has a PAR of 0.9 (Standard) or 1.2 (Widescreen).

2   PAL DVD video has a PAR of 1.066 (Standard) or 1.422 (Widescreen).

Pixel Aspect Ratio = Width / Height

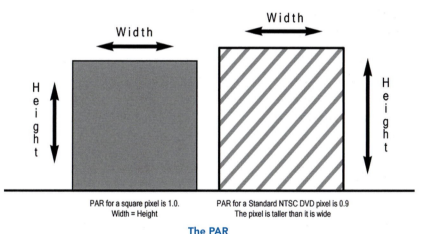

PAR for a square pixel is 1.0.   PAR for a Standard NTSC DVD pixel is 0.9
Width = Height   The pixel is taller than it is wide

The PAR

For video assets, Encore determines the PAR of the asset on import and sets the screen aspect ratio accordingly. If Encore can't properly determine the PAR of a video asset, then you can set the PAR manually by using the File ▶ Interpret Footage command.

You can mix video assets with different PARs in your project. For example, you could have a Standard PAR introduction video for your DVD, and have a Widescreen PAR main program.

Audio Assets

Encore can import audio in several different formats. These include:

1   Windows Audio files (.wav and .wma)

2   Dolby Digital audio (.ac3)

3   DTS digital audio (.dts)

4   Apple Macintosh audio (.aif and .aiff)

5   QuickTime audio (.mov)

6   MPEG audio (.mpg, .m2p and .mp3).

Although you can work with any of these audio formats while you are creating your project, Encore will convert all audio that isn't PCM audio (in the form of a .wav file), Dolby Digital audio or MPEG audio into one of those three formats when the DVD is built. Go to Edit ▶ Preferences ▶ Encoding to set the audio encoding scheme that will be used. The exception is DTS audio – it will be left unaltered by Encore and written to disc exactly as it was imported. And don't be alarmed if you import DTS audio into Encore and can't hear it while you preview your project. Adobe Encore DVD 2.0 will import DTS audio correctly and write DTS audio correctly out to disc, but preview of DTS audio inside of Encore is not supported.

Adobe Encore DVD 2.0 will produce finished disc with 16-bit, 48-kHz audio. If your source audio doesn't match that bit depth and sampling rate, Encore will have to resample the audio when the DVD is built. If you have a dedicated audio-editing program like Adobe Audition, it is best to prepare your audio assets in that program prior to importing them into Encore. For example, Encore has to resample CD audio from 44 to 48 kHz when the DVD is built. Since this resampling is unavoidable, using the tools in an external audio-editing program should allow you to retain more of the original sound quality.

Note: Support for MPEG-1, Layer II audio in NTSC DVD players is not required by the DVD specification. Since adding this support is optional for DVD player manufacturers, if you build an NTSC DVD using MPEG audio, you run the risk of drastically limiting the number of DVD players that will play the disc.

Graphic Assets

As with video and audio assets, Encore can import several graphic and picture file formats. These may be used as part of a slideshow or as objects in a menu. Still-image files do not require transcoding. The allowable formats include:

1   Photoshop files (.psd)

2   Windows bitmap files (.bmp)

3   Macintosh native picture format files (.pict)

4   Cross-platform compressed and uncompressed files (.png, .tiff, .tga, .jpg and .gif).

Importing Assets

In "The Project: Planning", I mentioned that proper planning begins with making a list of assets that you want to include in your program. The example flowchart from that chapter is the list that we will use to decide which assets should be imported into our project. Once they are inside of Encore, we can begin to assemble our program.

Encore provides four ways to import assets into a project:

1   Import as Asset

2   Import as Menu

3   Import as Slideshow

4   Import as Timeline.

You can use any of these import options at any time. The import option you select will be dictated by the type of assets to be imported or by the current project task. We will use different options as we import assets for our project.

The Import as Asset Command

It is generally best to import files as assets only if those files will ultimately be used as program material. Importing video files, audio files and slideshow images as assets works very well, but graphics and other images that are intended to be objects in the project's menus should be added to Encore's library instead of being imported as assets. We'll discuss why this is and how to add things to the Library in "The Project: Menu Design and Creation". To import a file as an asset:

1 Select File ▶ Import As ▶ Asset (Ctrl+I).

2 In the dialog that appears, navigate to the place on your hard drive where the file you want to import is located. Select it and click Open.

3 Encore will list the new asset in the lower section of the Project panel.

4 Select the new asset in the lower section of the Project panel to display a preview thumbnail and some key details about the file in the top section.

You can import several assets at once. If you import a lot of assets, it is a good idea to start organizing them right away. This is another example of how a good flowchart comes in handy; you can organize your assets according to how they will appear and be used in the program. For our project, we will put all of the assets for the Main Menu into one folder in the Project panel, and all of the assets for the Extras Menu in another. To create a new folder in the Project panel:

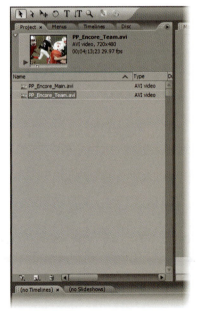

1 At the bottom of the Project panel, click the "Create a new item" button

2 Choose Folder

3 Enter a name for the new folder when prompted.

The Import as Timeline Command

If you know the file that you are importing will be used as part of your

The Project panel showing the imported assets in the lower section and the preview thumbnail image with file information in the top section

main program, then you can save a few steps by importing it as a timeline. The Import as Timeline command works best for importing video and audio files; it has limited usefulness for importing image files. To import a file as a timeline:

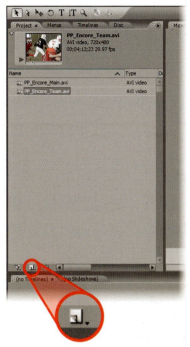

1 Select File ▶ Import As ▶ Timeline (Shift+Ctrl+T).

2 Select the file you want to import and click Open. Encore will automatically:
   • Add the file to the project both as an asset and as a new timeline. The new timeline will appear in the Project panel with the same name as the imported file.
   • Open a new Timeline viewer or add a new tab to an already-open Timeline viewer.

The Create a new item button

   • Add the imported asset to the new timeline and bring the Monitor panel forward with the first frame of the timeline displayed.

If program video and program audio are in separate files, importing them together as a timeline is especially handy; the new timeline will contain both the audio and the video, and it will be named for the video file that was part of the import.

Note: This feature only applies to a single video and a single audio file. If you import more than one video and audio file together, then Encore will put each imported file into a separate timeline.

The Import as Slideshow Command

If you want to make a slideshow part of your DVD project, then you can import one or more image files as an Encore slideshow. Gather all of the photos and

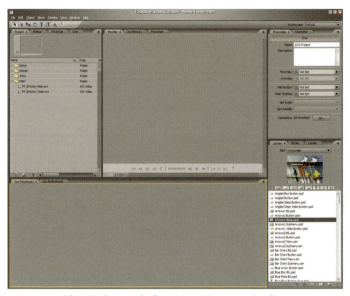

The Workspace before importing as a timeline

The Workspace after importing as a timeline

graphics that will be part of the slideshow together in a single folder on your hard drive. Then when you import, you will be able to select all of them at once and they will be added to the new slideshow. Our project includes a slideshow, so we will import our images this way. To import one or more image files as a slideshow:

1   Select File ► Import As ► Slideshow (Shift+Ctrl+G).

2   Select the files you want to import and click Open. Encore will automatically:

- Add the files to the Project panel as assets.
- Create a new slideshow and add the files to the slideshow.
- Bring a new Slideshow viewer and the Monitor panel to the front and display the first slide in the slideshow.

The Workspace after importing as a slideshow

As with importing a video file and an audio file together as a timeline, Encore has a cool feature that lets you import your images and a single audio file as a slideshow. The audio file will be added automatically as background audio for the slideshow when it is imported. To take advantage of this feature, you will need to put the audio file in the same folder as the images before you import.

The Import as Menu Command

Commercial and other experienced DVD authors often know exactly how they want their menus to look before they begin assembling them in a DVD authoring program like Encore. The program content will drive their menu design decisions. They create the graphics for the background and the other menu objects in another program before they begin to author the DVD. All that remains is for them to import the assembled graphics into Encore so they can become part of the disc's menu system.

The Workspace after importing as a menu

Adobe Encore DVD 2.0 supports this kind of flexibility for graphics that are saved as Adobe Photoshop (.psd) files. To import a graphic file as a menu:

1 Select File ▶ Import As ▶ Menu (Shift+Ctrl+I).

2 Encore adds the graphic file to the Project panel as a menu and opens a new Menu viewer.

A Second Look at the Project Panel

No matter how you import your files, it is important to check the details of each asset and each project element to ensure that everything was imported correctly. After import, Encore displays these details in the Project panel.

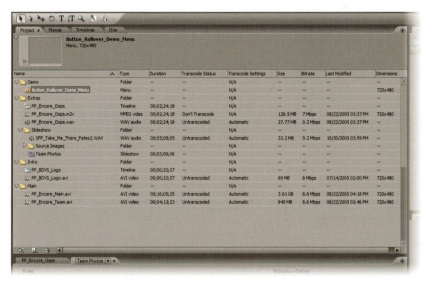

Check the details in the project panel after import

The Project panel also displays icons unique to each type of asset and element to provide quick identification for project operations. It's important to become familiar with these icons because they help readily differentiate between assets and project elements that may share a common name. They also play a big role in the Flowchart panel. We'll take a close look at the Flowchart panel in "The Project: Linking Everything Together".

Icons for assets and project elements

Locating and Replacing Assets

Sometimes, files that were in one place on your system yesterday are not in that same place today. You may have moved them to a newer, roomier hard disk or reorganized your folders to make it easier to find files. You may even have deleted them. Regardless of what caused the change, assets that have been imported into Encore are suddenly not where Encore expects them to be. When you open a project that contains these assets, Encore will ask you where they are. You will be presented with the Locate Asset dialog, which has the name of the missing file in the titlebar. You have a few choices:

1 You can navigate to the asset's new location and click Select. You must save the project to force Encore to remember this new location.

2 You can substitute a generic placeholder for the asset by clicking Skip. If you save the project and re-open it later, Encore will ask you about the missing asset again. Clicking Cancel effectively does the same thing.

3   You can substitute a permanent generic placeholder for the asset by clicking Offline. This tells Encore not to worry about the missing asset. If you save and then re-open the project, Encore won't ask you about it again.

The Locate Asset dialog

If you want to re-link an offline asset later on, you can open the Locate Asset dialog by selecting File ▶ Locate Asset (Shift+Ctrl+H). Navigate to the asset and click Select to tell Encore the new location.

Note: One word of caution here. Encore creates a project file and a project folder when you save a project. You should always consider them inseparable. You should probably consider them immovable as well. Unlike moving assets around, separating or moving the Encore project file and the project folder can wreak havoc with Encore's project references. Don't do it. You could end up with a corrupted project that will no longer open. Choose your Save location wisely.

If you author DVDs for clients that consistently have the same form and layout, for example, making archival DVDs of church services from week to week, then you probably are looking for a way to use one project as a template for future projects. Or, perhaps you decide that an asset currently being used in a project needs to be replaced by an updated version. With Adobe Encore DVD 2.0, you can easily insert new video and audio into existing timelines and menus by replacing their assets.

Encore is a very powerful tool for asset replacement. It doesn't matter, for example, if the original asset is an .avi file and you want to swap it out for an .mpg file. Encore knows what to do. The only restriction is that you can't replace an asset that contains audio with one that doesn't, or vice versa. To replace an asset:

1 In the Project panel, select the asset that you want to replace.

2 Go to File ▶ Replace Asset (Ctrl+H).

3 Navigate to the new asset's location and click Open.

Encore will import the new asset and replace all instances of the old asset in the project with the new one.

THE PROJECT:

Transcoding

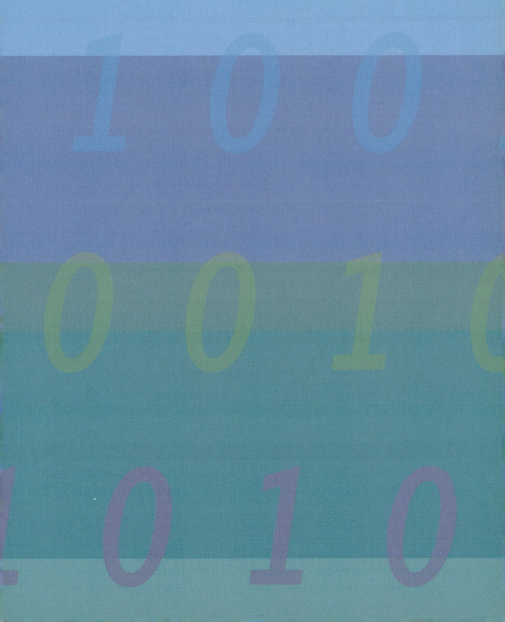

Welcome to the chapter about what many consider to be the Black Magic of DVD authoring: transcoding. We're going to take a short tour of this seemingly mystical art and show you how to penetrate the fog of mystery quickly and easily using the tools that are available right within Adobe Encore DVD 2.0.

Transcoding is the process that Encore uses to turn non-DVD-compliant assets into assets that match the worldwide DVD standard. What that really means is that all the video, audio and graphics files that you want to become part of your DVD must be transformed into assets that can fit on a blank DVD and then be displayed on a TV by any DVD player in the world. Think about transcoding this way:

1 Transcoding shrinks huge video and audio files so that they can fit on a blank DVD.

2 Transcoding ensures that the shrunken files can be played back by any DVD player.

The mysterious part of transcoding is how to shrink the video and audio so that when the finished disc is played back, the quality of the picture and sound is good enough to make the audience go "Oooh" and "Aaah" instead of "Ewww" and "Gross".

The simplest solution to this mystery is to let Encore keep the Transcode Settings for each asset at Automatic. This is the default setting and it is applied to each asset upon import.

Asset transcode settings set to Automatic

With the Automatic setting, Encore continually recalculates the total disc space required for the project, adjusting the Transcode Settings as content is added to the program in order to maintain the highest video and audio quality while making sure that everything will fit on the disc. These calculations occur behind-the-scenes and require no user input.

But before you can rely on Encore's automatic transcoding, you need to tell Encore what kind of blank DVD you will be using. There are two types of blank media that are widely available today: single layer and dual layer. Here are the capacities of each:

1 A single-layer disc, or *DVD-5,* can hold 4.7 gigabytes (GB) of data.

2 A dual-layer disc, or *DVD-9,* can hold 8.54 GB of data.

Select the Disc panel and choose the disc capacity from the drop-down box next to the disc graphic. If your finished project will be put on a DVD-5 disc, select 4.7 GB. If your project will be put on a DVD-9 disc, choose 8.54 GB. The default is 4.7 GB. We will put our finished project on a 4.7 GB DVD-5 disc.

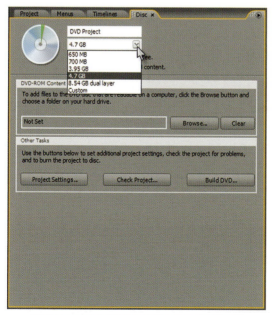

Make sure to tell encore the correct size of your blank media

Now look at the whole top section of the Disc panel: Encore gives both a graphical and a numerical indication of used and free space. In the disc graphic, the space required for assets that need to be transcoded is shown in red, and the space required for assets that have already been transcoded is shown in green. The space required for untranscoded assets is only an estimate; Encore won't know the exact size of a transcoded asset until transcoding is complete. The estimate is a good one, however, and you can count on its accuracy. Encore updates the space required whenever menus, timelines or slideshows are added to or deleted from the project.

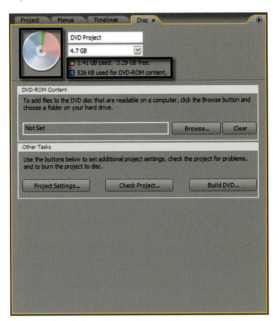

The Disc panel showing a graphical and numerical representation of the disc space used for the project so far

Transcode Settings

As good as it is, automatic transcoding is not a panacea. So when would you want to abandon Encore's automatic transcoding logic?

If you are planning to put your project on a dual-layer DVD-9 disc, then the answer is probably, "Never". The space available on a DVD-9 translates into a 2-hour or longer main program, plus plenty of supplemental material, all transcoded at the highest possible quality. For DVD-9, therefore, transcoding is essentially a set-it-and-forget-it operation. And since Encore chooses the Automatic setting by default when an asset is imported, you can even skip the set-it part!

However, many authors began with, and are still heavily invested in DVD-5. The most common situation requiring a solution other than automatic transcoding would be a very long program that is to be authored on a DVD-5 disc.

The 4.7 GB storage limit for a DVD-5 can present a problem for DVD authors if the total time for all the program material on the disc exceeds approximately one and one-half hours. For total program times less than that, a normal DVD-5 disc can hold all of the program material transcoded with outstanding video and audio quality. Discs produced at this high-quality setting will be virtually indistinguishable from the original source video and audio.

Once the total program time exceeds one and one-half hours on a DVD-5 disc though, compromises must be made. These compromises will affect the video assets far more significantly than the audio assets. Encore's default audio transcoding scheme is Dolby Digital, which produces superb audio and very small file sizes. There are minimal space-saving benefits to adjusting the audio transcode settings, so we will focus on video transcoding.

The villain that steals your available disc space is an asset's *bit rate*. Bit rate is usually measured in megabits per second, or *Mbps*, and is a standard measure of video quality. Better quality is obtained by using higher bit rates when assets are transcoded. But higher bit rates also use up more disc space than lower bit rates do. With relatively short programs, running out of space on the disc is not an issue and Encore's automatic transcoding logic selects bit rates that are as high as possible to ensure quality that is as high as possible. But as program length gets longer and longer, automatic transcoding forces the bit rate lower and lower so that all the program material can still fit on the disc. At some point, the bit rate will get so low that the video quality is no longer acceptable.

Note: Encore's automatic transcoding is smart about low bit rates, too. Encore will not automatically transcode any video asset at a bit rate below a certain threshold, even if the disc capacity is exceeded. Instead, Encore will refuse to build the project or burn the disc. But don't fret about Encore's obstinate attitude;

that threshold level is so low that no one would want to watch the resulting video anyway.

So what can you do to ensure acceptable video and audio quality on a DVD-5 when your program is long? The answer has three parts:

1 Vary how each asset is transcoded.

2 Determine the number of *passes*, or how many times Encore gets to examine the asset frame-by-frame.

3 Choose which assets will be transcoded at higher bit rates and which ones will be transcoded at lower bit rates.

In Encore, you have two choices for how an asset will be transcoded: Constant Bit Rate (CBR) or Variable Bit Rate (VBR). CBR transcoding will transcode the entire asset at the same bit rate. VBR transcoding will transcode the asset at an average bit rate. VBR transcoding looks at the amount of detail and picture information in each frame of the asset as it goes along, varying the bit rate as necessary between set maximum and minimum values to maintain the best picture quality and the selected average bit rate. This analysis makes VBR slower than CBR. The advantage of using VBR is that, at lower bit rates, the video quality of the transcoded file will usually be noticeably better than the same file transcoded using CBR. At higher bit rates, there isn't much difference in the video quality between assets transcoded with VBR and those transcoded with CBR.

Encore offers one-pass or two-pass transcoding. One-pass or two-pass defines whether you give the transcoder one or two chances to examine the asset frame-by-frame. If you choose two-pass, the transcoder will use the information from the first pass to refine its bit rate decisions during the second pass. Although it takes twice as long, choosing two-pass can further increase the video quality of the transcoded asset.

Note: Reserve two-pass transcoding for VBR. Two-pass doesn't make sense for CBR transcoding.

For parts one and two of the answer above, the choices are relatively straightforward: if you want to maximize quality, and at the same time minimize file size by using lower bit rates, choose two-pass VBR transcoding. But what about part three? How do we choose which assets should get transcoded at higher bit rates and which ones get transcoded at lower bit rates?

The answer is in the assets themselves. Video assets that have lots of motion across the frame, or lots of fine detail like forest scenes or scenes with water surfaces, are very challenging for any transcoder and require higher bit rates than other video assets. Keeping this in mind, you can choose to lower the bit rate for video assets that don't have a lot of motion, or are less detailed. This allows you to increase the bit rate for more challenging video assets, thereby preserving the overall quality of the whole program.

So now we need to reach into Encore's toolbox for transcoding presets that are easy to use and will produce good results. Here's how to get to them:

1 In the Project panel, right-click an asset that needs transcoding.

2 Select Transcode Settings.

3 Select the preset that you want to use.

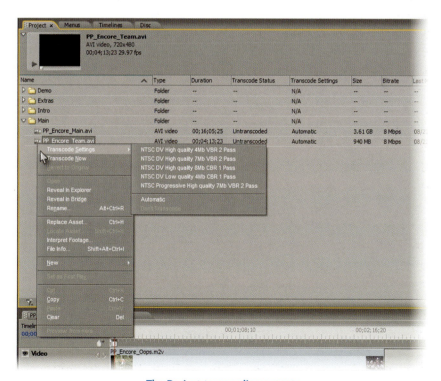

The Project transcoding presets

Apply these presets to your troublesome video assets and you will achieve maximum video quality in the minimum amount of space.

Transcoding Assets Within Encore

Once Encore knows what Transcode Settings to use for each asset, the actual transcoding can take place. All non-DVD-compliant assets have to be transcoded before the project can be built or burned to disc. Transcoding can take a lot of time, especially if you use two-pass VBR transcoding for large projects. It can be frustrating to tell Encore to begin building or burning the project, only to have to wait for any non-compliant assets to be transcoded. Adobe Encore DVD 2.0 makes *background transcoding* available to ease the pain of this time-consuming task. With background transcoding, you can tell Encore to transcode assets early on in the project while you continue to work on other tasks. To take advantage of background transcoding:

1 Select an asset in the Project panel.

2 Right-click on the asset and choose Transcode Now.

3 Encore automatically opens the Progress panel and begins transcoding the asset.

There is no "free lunch", however; background transcoding takes up memory and CPU cycles, which will slow down your system somewhat. Having a computer that exceeds the recommended system specifications for Encore will minimize any impact to your system from background transcoding.

The Progress panel after selecting Transcode Now

Transcoding an asset will create a new file on your hard drive. When transcoding is complete, Encore points to the new, transcoded asset in the Project panel. The original file is left unchanged. If you ever decide that you need to transcode the original file in a different way, Encore allows you to revert to the original file. To Revert to Original:

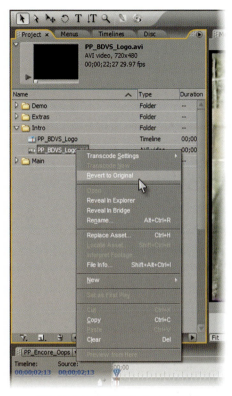

1   Right-click on the asset in the Project panel.

2   Choose Revert to Original.

Transcoding Assets Before Import

Another way you can save time on transcoding in Encore is to ensure that any assets that are imported into Encore are already DVD-compliant. For example, instead of exporting your movie from a non-linear editor, or *NLE*, as an .avi file or .mov file (both of which will

The Revert to Original command

need to be transcoded by Encore), you might consider taking advantage of your NLE's own transcoding capabilities to export a DVD-compliant video. When that asset is brought into Encore, it will not need to be transcoded.

There are two main drawbacks to transcoding outside of Encore:

1   You have to make all the transcoding decisions yourself. You can't take advantage of Encore's automatic transcoding or built-in presets.

2   Chapter point placement inside of Encore is less precise with material that has been transcoded outside of Encore. We will talk about adding chapter points in "The Project: Timeline Creation".

There is another, more subtle, issue that can affect you if you transcode your assets external to Encore. Blank DVD disc capacities are listed in *Gigabytes*, or billions of bytes, and are abbreviated as GB. The capacity of a DVD-5 disc is 4.7 GB, or 4,700,000,000 bytes. If we write that number using powers of ten, it becomes 4.7×10^9 bytes. However, not all gigabytes are the same. Computer operating systems like Microsoft Windows calculate file sizes based on powers of two, not powers of ten like we just did. For example, you and I would think of a kilobyte as 1000 bytes, or 10^3 bytes. A computer thinks of a kilobyte as 2^{10} bytes, or 1024 bytes. This difference between human thinking and computer thinking increases as file sizes get bigger and bigger. A file on your computer's hard disk that would occupy the same space as a blank DVD-5 would be listed in Windows Explorer as 4.37 GB. As silly as it sounds, the end result is that you can't fit 4.7 GB of transcoded assets on an empty 4.7 GB DVD disc! For dual-layer discs, you can only fit 7.95 GB of transcoded assets on an 8.54 GB blank DVD-9.

The good news is that Adobe Encore DVD 2.0 reports file sizes in millions or billions of normal human bytes, not computer bytes, so that you don't have to worry about this discrepancy. Once you import your DVD-compliant assets into Encore and create project elements with them, you can use the Project, Disc and Timeline panels as tools to judge exactly how much space they will take up on the finished DVD.

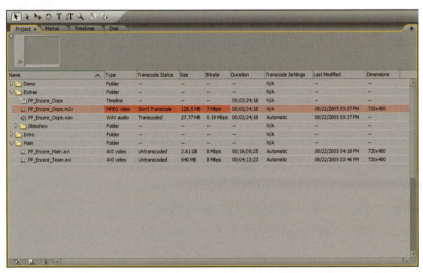

Encore shows the bit rate and transcoded file size for an asset transcoded external to Encore

THE PROJECT:

Timeline Creation

Creating timelines is critical to the DVD authoring process inside of Adobe Encore DVD 2.0. Timelines are the building blocks of your project. You can't background transcode an asset or see how much space an asset will occupy on disc until it's added to a timeline. Menu buttons can only point to assets if they are part of a timeline. Timelines can only link to assets that are part of another timeline. To paraphrase an old song: an asset is nobody until somebody adds it to a timeline.

In Encore, a timeline can contain video, audio and still image assets. A special type of timeline that can contain only still images and audio is called a *slideshow*. We will look at how to work with timelines first, and then we'll see how to create and work with slideshows.

The Timeline Editing Workspace

For the first part of this discussion, we will use one of the workspace presets that shipped with Adobe Encore DVD 2.0: the Timeline Editing workspace. To access the Timeline Editing workspace do one of the following:

1 Select Window ▶ Workspace ▶ Timeline Editing.

2 From the Workspace drop-down menu in the Toolbar, choose Timeline Editing.

Notice the five panels that have been brought forward in their frames: Project, Monitor, Properties, the Timeline Viewer and Timelines. These panels provide useful information about the timelines you create and they provide easy access to the controls that you need when working with timelines.

Creating a Timeline

In "The Project: Importing Assets" we saw that using the Import As Timeline command creates timelines when you import. At some point, however, you will likely have individual assets already in the Project panel that need to be added to a timeline. You can create an empty timeline and then drag-and-drop assets into it or you can highlight the asset(s) in the Project panel that you want to be in the timeline and then create it with those selected assets. Either way, the process is

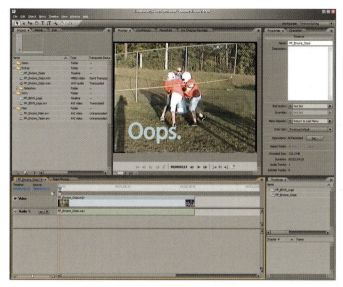

The Timeline Editing workspace

the same. To create a new timeline, start with the Project panel forward in its frame and do one of the following:

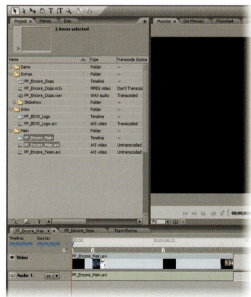

1 Select File ▶ New and choose Timeline (Ctrl+T).

2 Right-click the asset or a blank area in the Project panel and select New ▶ Timeline.

3 Click the New Item button at the bottom of the Project panel and choose Timeline.

Similar to what happens when you import using the Import As Timeline command, if you

The highlighted asset and the new timeline

highlight exactly one video asset and one audio asset in the Project panel and then create a new timeline, it will contain the video asset in the video track and the audio asset in the audio track. The new timeline will be named for the video asset. If you highlight more than one video asset or more than one audio asset before you create your new timeline, then Encore will create separate timelines automatically for each individual asset.

The Timeline Viewer

Let's take a closer look at the Timeline viewer. In the left-hand pane of the viewer you will find the track headers for the Video and Audio tracks and the readouts for the Timeline and Source *timecodes*. In Adobe Encore DVD 2.0, timecode is always represented as hours:minutes:seconds:frames.

Across the top of the Timeline viewer is the *time ruler*. The blue wedge icon in the time ruler that is attached to the red vertical cursor is known as the *Current Time Indicator*, or *CTI*. The exact position of the CTI along the time ruler is always indicated by the Timeline and Source timecode readouts.

The space in the tracks underneath the time ruler is where the timeline's assets will appear. Video assets are represented as blue segments with a small thumbnail image of the beginning frame of the asset and a thumbnail of the ending frame, one at each end of the segment. Audio assets appear as green segments with no thumbnails.

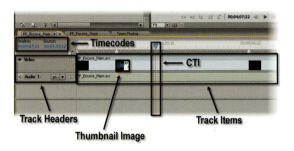

Navigating in the Timeline Viewer

If you want to see more or less of your timeline in the Timeline viewer, zoom in or out using the Zoom slider at the bottom left of the track header pane. Zooming is also accomplished using the (+) and (−) keys on the numeric keypad or above the letter P on the keyboard. Be sure to try out these two keyboard

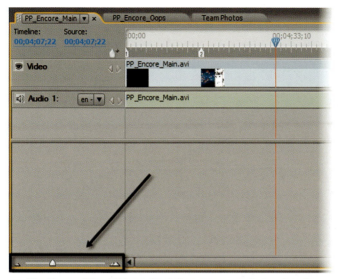

The Zoom slider. Slide to the left to zoom out (−) and to the right to zoom in (+)

shortcuts; they will speed up your work in Encore significantly while you work with timelines.

When the zoom level is where you want it, move other parts of the timeline into view by using the scrollbar at the bottom of the viewer.

Here are some ways to get where you want to go in the timeline:

1   Drag the head of the CTI left or right to *scrub* in the Timeline viewer. Scrubbing advances or rewinds the playback of the timeline using the speed at which you drag the CTI.

2   Use the (Left Arrow) and (Right Arrow) keys on your keyboard to step through the timeline frame-by-frame, either forward or backward.

3   Click in the time ruler. The CTI will jump to where you clicked.

4   Scrub the *hot text* in the Timeline or Source timecode readouts. The hot text is highlighted in a bright color (either blue or orange, depending on the Interface Brightness setting) and is underlined by a dotted line.

5 Click on a timecode readout to directly enter a timecode. Press (Enter).

6 To move the CTI quickly to the beginning or the end of the timeline, use the (Home) or (End) keys.

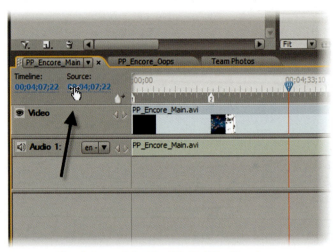

Ready to scrub hot text in the Timeline viewer

The Monitor Panel

The Monitor panel lets you watch the playback of a timeline or a slideshow. To start and stop playback:

1 Click the Play button at the bottom of the panel to begin full-speed playback. Once playback begins, the Play button changes to a Pause button. Click the Pause button to stop playback.

2 Use the (Spacebar) to start and stop playback from the keyboard.

The timecode of the current position of the CTI is displayed adjacent to the Play/Pause button.

Note: There is no Fast Forward, Rewind or Reverse Play capability in the Monitor panel. Scrub in the Timeline viewer to simulate these operations. As you scrub, you will get an audio and video preview in the Monitor panel.

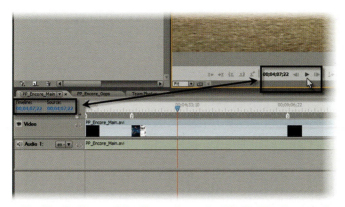

The Play button and the timecode readout in the Monitor panel

The quality of the display in the Monitor panel is determined by the settings in Edit ▶ Preferences ▶ General ▶ Playback Quality. Here is what you will see for each of the three available modes:

- High: Display during playback and while paused will be at full resolution.

- Draft: Display during playback and while paused will be at quarter resolution.

- Automatic: Uses Draft display quality during playback and High display quality when paused.

At the High playback quality setting, interlaced video is displayed using both fields. Automatic displays both interlaced fields only during Pause. On a computer monitor, interlacing artifacts, or *combing*, may be present if:

1 The zoom level is 100%. And

2 Interlaced video is played back using the High setting. Or

3 The CTI is paused over a scene with a lot of cross-frame motion using the High or Automatic settings.

At the Draft setting, interlaced video is displayed only during playback. When paused, the video will be de-interlaced and only one of the two fields shown. This eliminates any interlacing artifacts.

Note: At zoom settings other than 100%, combing will not be seen no matter which playback quality setting is used.

Interlacing artifacts, or combing, in the Monitor panel

Adding Chapter Markers

Ever since VCRs became available to the average consumer, there has been one drawback to watching videotapes that has annoyed everyone at some point: you can't watch the really good parts, or even watch the whole video again, without having to wait for the Fast Forward or Rewind controls to shuttle the tape to right spot. The DVD format has solved that problem by allowing discs to be created with *chapter markers*. A chapter marker is a navigation point that tells a DVD player what part of the program to play next. A DVD author will add chapter markers to let the viewer quickly navigate to the different scenes that make up the story or to other important points in the program. All timelines in Encore have at least one chapter marker – the beginning of the timeline.

Note: You cannot move or delete the first chapter marker of a timeline.

To add a chapter marker to a timeline:

1 Navigate to the place in the timeline where you want to add the chapter.

2 Click on the Add Chapter button (* on the Numeric Keypad).

The first chapter marker in a timeline

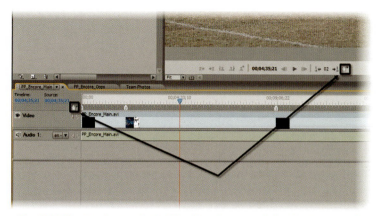

The Add Chapter button in the Timeline viewer and the Monitor panel

Setting a Poster Frame

When a chapter marker is added to a timeline, Encore also creates a thumbnail image in the Timeline viewer using a frame of video that represents the marker. These thumbnail images in the Timeline viewer are called *poster frames.*

Poster frames help the DVD author, and the audience, quickly identify project elements and chapters. Poster frames in the Timeline viewer and in the element icons in the Flowchart panel assist the author, while poster frames in Video Thumbnail buttons on menus on the finished DVD help the audience quickly locate scenes and chapters. We'll discuss the Flowchart panel and Video Thumbnail buttons in "The Project: Linking Everything Together".

A chapter marker and its poster frame

Poster frames are properties of chapter markers; you can only set a poster frame when a chapter marker is selected in the Timeline viewer. To set the poster frame for a chapter marker:

1 Bring the Properties panel forward in its frame.

2 Select the chapter marker for which you want to set a poster frame. The chapter marker turns red to indicate that it is selected.

3 Navigate in the Timeline viewer to the timecode that represents the video frame that you want to use as a poster frame. You can use any frame in the timeline for the poster frame; there are no restrictions.

4 Right-click the CTI and choose Set Poster Frame (Shift+*).

5 Encore creates the poster frame, adds a poster frame icon for the selected chapter to the timeline, and updates the poster frame timecode in the Properties panel.

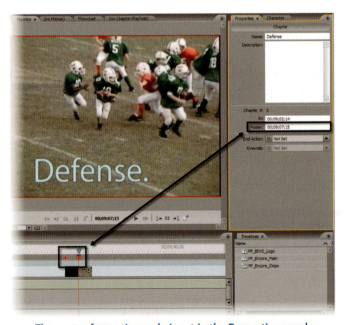

The poster frame timecode is set in the Properties panel

If you add a chapter marker to a timeline, and the video frame that corresponds to the chapter marker's timecode is black, Encore will automatically generate a poster frame for that chapter marker at the first bright frame after the marker. The most common situation where this occurs is when a fade-to-black transition is used between scenes in a video asset.

Note: If the first bright frame after the chapter marker lies more than 5 seconds beyond the marker, then Encore will abandon its attempt to find a bright frame. Instead, the poster frame for the marker will be shown as a frame of black video. In this case, you will need to set the poster frame for the chapter marker manually.

Transcoded Assets and Chapter Markers

For untranscoded assets, Encore will let you add chapter markers at the exact frame that you want. If an asset has been transcoded already, however, your choice of where to place the chapter marker is more limited.

Because of the way that assets are transcoded to conform to the worldwide DVD standard, you can only place a chapter marker at certain frames in a transcoded asset. Adobe Encore DVD 2.0 indicates those frames with tick marks along the bottom edge of the time ruler. The tick marks are close enough in time that you have to be zoomed into the timeline to see them. Zoom in (+) to a timeline that contains a transcoded asset until you can see these tick marks. Each tick mark indicates a legal position for a chapter marker. If you try and add a chapter marker in between these locations, Encore will choose the closest legal position prior to the CTI.

These tick marks
indicate legal
chapter marker
locations for
transcoded assets

Navigation Using Chapter Markers

Once you have chapter markers placed in your timeline, you can easily navigate from chapter to chapter. To navigate the timeline quickly using chapter markers:

1 Click on the Previous Chapter button (Page Up) in the Monitor panel.

2 Click on the Next Chapter button (Page Down) in the Monitor panel.

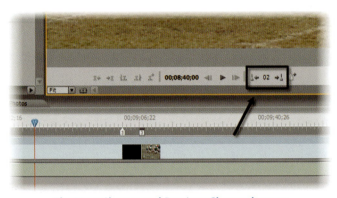

The Next Chapter and Previous Chapter buttons

Adding Audio Tracks

If you want to add a soundtrack for a director's commentary or a different language audio track, you need to add new audio tracks to your timeline. To add a new audio track to a timeline:

1 Right-click inside the Timeline viewer's track area.

2 Choose Add Audio Track.

3 Drag-and-drop audio assets into the new track.

Note: Unlike a video or audio editing application, only one audio track at a time can be active in Encore. For example, you can't have the director's commentary by itself on one audio track, the video soundtrack on another audio track and then have the DVD player play both tracks at the same time to get the commentary over the soundtrack. Instead, you have to mix down the

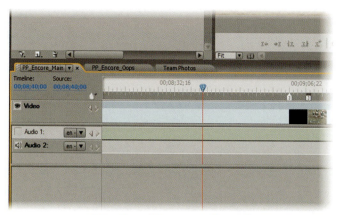

A timeline with a new audio track

commentary and the soundtrack in a video or audio editing application and then bring that mixed-down audio asset into Encore for use as the commentary track.

If you create multilingual DVDs or DVDs with audio commentary frequently, then you can return to Edit ▶ Preferences ▶ Timeline and set the default number of audio tracks to a number that best suits your needs. Once you make that change, all new timelines that you create, by any method, will contain that number of audio tracks.

Adding Subtitles

Another way to break the language barrier of your program material is by adding *subtitles*. A subtitle is text that is overlaid on video. Even if you don't need a text translation of the scene dialog, be aware that subtitles can also be used to assist the hearing impaired, to give supplemental information to the audience or to provide sing-along lyrics for a music video. Before you can add subtitles, however, you need to create at least one subtitle track. To add a subtitle track to your timeline:

1 Right-click in the track area of the timeline.

2 Choose Add Subtitle track.

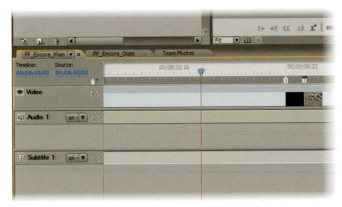

A timeline with a new subtitle track

Note: As with additional audio tracks, only one subtitle track can be active at a time. Unlike layered tracks in video editing applications, you can't composite subtitle tracks in Encore.

You add subtitles to a subtitle track either by typing in the Monitor panel with the Text tool or importing a subtitle script.

To add subtitles by typing in the Monitor panel:

1 Position the CTI in the Timeline viewer where you want your subtitle to begin.

2 Click on the Monitor tab to bring it forward in its frame.

3 Select the Text tool from the Toolbar (T).

4 Turn on the Monitor panel's Safe Area display.

The Monitor panel with the Safe Area display and the Show Safe Area button

5   Click in the Monitor panel inside the inner rectangle, or Title Safe Area, and begin typing.

6   Click anywhere outside the Monitor panel or press (Esc) to create the subtitle.

Note: Keeping your subtitles within the Title Safe Area is critical to ensure that your subtitles can be seen on any display device. A deeper discussion of the importance of the Safe Area display can be found in "The Project: Menu Design and Creation".

Each new subtitle that you create will have a length of time as determined by the default subtitle length setting in Edit ▶ Preferences ▶ Timelines. Since you probably won't want all your subtitles to be the same length, you can easily change the length of the subtitle. To make a subtitle that is already in the timeline longer:

1   Move the CTI to where you want the subtitle to end.

2   Zoom in to the timeline until the gray subtitle segment is large enough for you to see how long it is by referencing the time ruler and you can read a few words of the subtitle text on the segment. A light gray segment indicates that the subtitle is not selected; dark gray indicates the subtitle is selected.

3   Hover the cursor over the right edge of the subtitle clip. The cursor will change to the Trim tool – a red bracket with a double-headed arrow through its middle.

4   Change the length of the subtitle by dragging the Trim tool until the right edge of the subtitle clip lines up with the CTI.

5   Because the edge of the subtitle clip will not "snap" to the CTI when you drag, you may have to zoom into the timeline all the way to get frame-accurate trimming of subtitle length.

Note: The DVD specification does not allow subtitles to cross chapter markers. If you trim a subtitle and it ends up crossing a chapter marker, Encore will automatically split the subtitle into two subtitles to conform to the DVD spec.

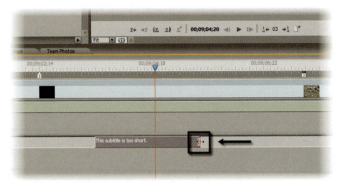

Trimming to make the subtitle longer

If you are making the subtitle shorter, then it's a little easier to get frame-accurate trimming. Here's how:

1 Move the CTI to where you want the subtitle to end.

2 Click the Trim Subtitle Out-Point to Here button in the Monitor panel.

The same adjustments to subtitle length can be made by trimming the subtitle's in point as well. And if the subtitle is the right length but in the wrong place, you can change the subtitle's location by dragging the clip left or right in the subtitle track.

To navigate from subtitle to subtitle:

1 Click on the Next Subtitle button (Page Up) in the Monitor panel.

2 Click on the Previous Subtitle button (Page Down) in the Monitor panel.

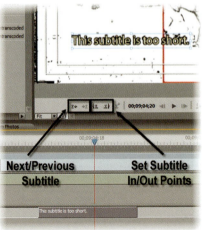

The subtitle navigation buttons in the Monitor panel

If you need a lot of subtitles in your program, you will quickly tire of typing in the Monitor panel. There is a better way to create subtitles and it's available at no cost. The

freeware application, "Subtitle Workshop" is available at http://www.urusoft.net/
products.php?cat=sw&lang=1 and it offers advanced subtitle editing capabilities
and a wide range of export options. The subtitle scripts exported from Subtitle
Workshop can easily be imported into Encore. To import a subtitle script:

1   Right-click in the
track area of the
Timeline viewer.

2   Select Import
Subtitles.

3   Choose the type of
script you want to
import.

4   Navigate to, and
select, the subtitle
script. Click Open.

5   Select the options
you want for the
subtitle from the
Import Subtitles
dialog. If you are
new to working with
imported subtitles,
go ahead and accept
the defaults by clicking OK. You can easily change the way that the
subtitles look after they are imported. We'll see how to do that in the next
section, "Changing the Appearance of Subtitle Text".

**The Import Subtitles dialog shows the video frame
from the Timeline that corresponds to the starting
timecode of the first subtitle in the script**

6   The imported subtitles will automatically be placed inside the Title
Safe Area.

Changing the Appearance of Subtitle Text

Whether your subtitles were imported or typed, you may decide to change the
appearance of the text in the subtitle to make it more readable or to make it
easier for the audience to follow the on-screen dialog.

To have the maximum amount of control over the subtitle text, you will need to use a combination of two tools: the Character panel and the Timeline Color Set dialog. Changes you make using the Character panel affect any subtitles that are currently selected and all new subtitles. The Timeline Color Set dialog affects all subtitles in that timeline.

To use the Character panel to change the properties of the font:

1   Bring the Character panel forward in its frame by selecting the Character tab.

2   Select one or more subtitles to change. If you just want to change the appearance of new subtitles, you must deselect all existing subtitles first.

3   Make changes to the controls in the Character panel as desired. Not all of the controls apply to subtitles. For example, you can't change the color of the subtitle text using the Character panel. The Timeline Color Set controls the color of the subtitle text.

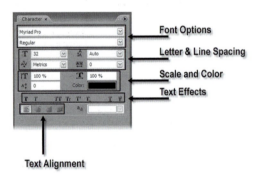

Font Options

Letter & Line Spacing

Scale and Color

Text Effects

Text Alignment

The Character panel showing the controls for changing individual properties of the font. Not all of the controls apply to subtitles

Note: For more details on the Character panel, refer to "The Project: Menu Design and Creation".

The Timeline Color Set dialog lets you change the color of the text. To change the color and style of the subtitle text:

1   Select Timeline ▶ Edit Timeline Color Set.

2   Click on the New Color Set button and then name the new color set. If you don't, you will be making changes to the Timeline Default color set, which will affect every timeline in the project.

3 Click on the color swatch of any color you want to change. New subtitles default to Subtitle Group 1. Set the desired color in the Color Picker dialog that appears.

4 Adjust the *opacity* of any of the colors by choosing an opacity setting from the drop-down list adjacent to that color. Opacity is the opposite of transparency. An object that is 100% transparent is invisible, but an object with 100% opacity is completely opaque. All Adobe applications use opacity settings to control transparency.

Because of the way that DVD players display subtitle text, the text itself can appear somewhat jagged. Choosing a proper color for the Anti-alias control minimizes this jagged appearance. Adobe Encore DVD 2.0 provides an easy way to get a good color choice for the Anti-alias control: in the Timeline Color Set dialog, select Create Anti-alias color from Fill and Stroke for the Subtitle Group that you want to Anti-alias.

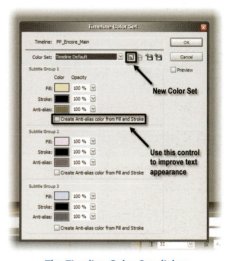

The Timeline Color Set dialog

Subtitles can be modified individually. Notice that each Timeline Color Set has three Subtitle Groups available. Each of these Subtitle Groups corresponds to a Highlight Group in the Properties panel. Assigning a different subtitle text color to different characters in a scene is a good way to help the viewer follow the dialog. To change the properties of individual subtitles:

1 Select the subtitles that you want to modify.

2 Click on the Properties tab to bring the Properties panel forward.

3 Use the Highlight Group, Stroke and Alignment controls to change the appearance and position of the subtitles.

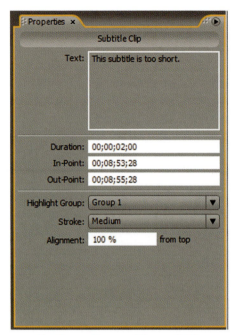

The Properties panel for a subtitle

Joining Assets in a Single Timeline

Recall from "The Project: Transcoding" that one way to ensure that all of your program material can fit on a single disc is to transcode less demanding clips at lower bit rates, preserving extra disc space for the higher bit rates that more demanding clips require. Adobe Encore DVD 2.0 has a new feature that will make this easier and more flexible than ever before. Once a timeline is created, you can place additional video and audio assets in the timeline, joining them seamlessly end-to-end in the same track.

If you have enough program material to be concerned about available space on the blank DVD, here's how to take advantage of this powerful new feature:

1   Divide the program material into segments in your non-linear editing program based on how demanding you think the video material is.

2   Export each of those segments individually to create separate files for them.

3   Import the separate files as assets into Encore.

4   Create an empty timeline.

5   Place the assets end-to-end in the new timeline to join them together and recreate the program as it existed in your non-linear editor (NLE).

6   Transcode each asset using different Encore presets as necessary.

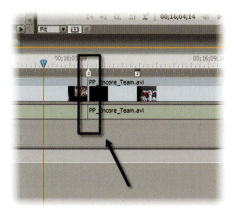

The Source timecode

With multiple assets in the same timeline, the separate Source timecode readout allows for quick navigation and accurate chapter placement within a particular asset.

Joining multiple assets together in one timeline. Note that a chapter point is automatically created where the assets are joined.

Seamlessly joining separate assets into a single timeline can also significantly speed up your workflow if you are gathering multiple assets from different sources to make up a single program. For seamless playback of multiple assets in earlier versions of Encore, you would have had to stitch all of the assets together in a non-linear editing program and then export them from the NLE as a single asset to be imported into Encore. Joining assets in a single timeline in Encore saves you the time that would otherwise have been spent in the NLE importing, editing and exporting the video assets.

Note: If your project contains assets with different pixel aspect ratios (PARs – see "The Project: Importing Assets"), they must be put into separate timelines. If you try to mix assets with different PARs in the same timeline, Encore will politely ignore your request when you try to drag the mismatched asset into the timeline.

The Slideshow Design Workspace

It's time to switch workspaces because the Timeline Editing workspace isn't very well suited to working with slideshows. To access the Slideshow Design workspace do one of the following:

1   Select Window ▶ Workspace ▶ Slideshow Design.

2   Select Slideshow Design from the Workspace drop-down menu in the Toolbar.

The Slideshow Design workspace

Adding Still Images and Audio to a Slideshow

If you imported your still images and audio together as a slideshow then you're ready to go. If you imported your still images and audio as assets, here's how to get them into a slideshow:

1 Select the images and audio assets you want to add to the slideshow. They will be added to the slideshow in the same order that they are sorted in the Project panel. Encore automatically creates a chapter point for each image that is added to the slideshow.

2 Select File ▶ New and choose Slideshow (Ctrl+G). Or

3 Right-click one of the images and select New ▶ Slideshow. Or

4 Click the New Item button at the bottom of the Project panel and choose Slideshow.

Note: Unlike an ordinary timeline, if you select multiple audio assets before you create your slideshow, all of the audio assets will get added to the slideshow.

Like the still image assets, they will be set up to play in sequence by the order that they are sorted in the Project panel. Since this may not be the order you want, and since there is no easy way to change the order of the audio assets in the Slideshow viewer, I recommend adding your audio assets to the slideshow one at a time, and in the order you want them to play.

The Slideshow Viewer

The Slideshow viewer is divided into two panes: Slides and Slideshow Options. If you've opened a Slideshow viewer and all you see are the slides, then the Options pane is hidden. To reveal it again, click on the Hide/Show arrow in the middle of the right-hand edge of the Slideshow viewer.

There is a zoom slider just like in the Timeline viewer. The (+) and (−) keyboard shortcuts work the same, too. As you zoom out, you will see more images in the viewer and each thumbnail will get smaller. As you zoom in, the thumbnails get bigger and you see fewer images at one time.

As with an ordinary timeline, you watch your slideshow and control playback in the Monitor panel. The (Spacebar) keyboard shortcut for starting and stopping playback works for the Slideshow viewer as well.

Click this arrow to reveal the Slideshow Options

Scaling Slideshow Images

Very rarely will the pictures in a slideshow fit the standard DVD frame size exactly. Encore handles this by *scaling* misfit images. Scaling an image zooms in or out on the image to make its height fit the frame from top to bottom or to make its width fit the frame from side to side. To set the scaling methods for one or more slides:

1 Select the slides in the Slideshow viewer.

2 Open the Scale drop-down list in the Properties panel and select one of the following:
- *Scale and Apply Matte* scales the image in its largest dimension, either height or width, and then adds a black matte to fill up any empty space that remains. This is the default setting.
- *Scale and Crop Edges* scales the image in its shortest dimension to fill the frame with the picture and then crops any part of the picture that falls outside the frame.
- *Do Nothing* leaves the image alone and fills any empty space with a black matte or crops any part of the picture that falls outside the frame.

Experiment with each of the scaling options; you can achieve quite different and dramatic results in the finished slideshow by changing them. There isn't really a best setting – which one you use will depend on the image itself and the creative expression that you have in mind for the show.

Widescreen Slideshows

Encore makes it very easy to set up your slideshow if you are authoring your DVD to be shown on a widescreen display:

1 Select the Slideshow (not just one of the slides) by clicking in the gray around a slide. You can also select the slideshow in the Project panel.

2 In the Properties panel, set the Aspect Ratio to 16:9 for widescreen.

Scale settings for individual slides in the Properties panel. The scale settings are not available for an image asset until it is added to a slideshow

3 Encore automatically changes the PAR of the still images to match the screen aspect ratio that you chose.

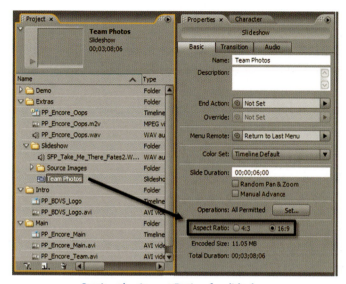

Setting the Aspect Ratio of a slideshow

Creating Your Slideshow

Old-time slide projectors once served a noble purpose – sharing your slides with family and friends. 35 mm slides were too hard to view on their own and it was too expensive to have copies printed for everyone. So the solution was to invite folks over for an evening of slide viewing where everyone could see the pictures at the same time as they were projected onto a wall or a screen.

Noble purpose or not, there was an almost inevitable result: audience boredom. Static images displayed without music or interesting commentary often gave guests a chance to catch up on their sleep. Well, not so anymore!

Adobe Encore DVD 2.0 provides a very easy and entertaining way to present your pictures in a DVD slideshow. Because of the way that Encore slideshows are transcoded, they also have a big space advantage over similar productions created in another application and then imported into Encore.

Enough introductions; let's get this (slide) show on the road!

Arranging the Slides

The first thing you should do is arrange the images in your slideshow. The Slides pane of the Slideshow viewer lays out your slides in much the same way that a Hollywood movie director lays out a storyboard. And just like that movie storyboard, you can arrange the slides so that they tell your story just the way you want. To arrange your slides in the Slideshow viewer:

1   Click on the Hide/Show arrow between the panes of the viewer to temporarily hide the Slideshow Options pane. This gives you more room in the viewer for your storyboard.

2   Zoom out so that you can see a reasonable number of slides, but not so far that the thumbnails are too small for you to work with.

3   When you find a slide that needs to be moved to a different position, drag it to its new location. Encore indicates where the slide will be dropped with a dark, vertical line that will appear in-between two slides.

4   Drop the slide. The rest of the slides in the show will shift automatically to accommodate the relocated slide.

Encore indicates the slide's drop location. Here, slide number 22 will be dropped between slides 18 and 19

You can add more slides to the show from the Project panel by dragging and dropping them into the Slides pane. Slides can be deleted as well.

Adding Effects and Transitions to the Slideshow

Once the slides are arranged the way you want, jazz up your slideshow with *effects* and *transitions*. Effects in Encore are motion based. You can have the image move, or *pan*, across the screen, zoom in or out, or pan and zoom together. Transitions change how the show gets from one image to the next. The most popular transition is the *Cross Dissolve*, where one image fades into the next.

One of the things that makes Adobe Encore DVD 2.0 such a powerful program is how easy it is to create a very professional-looking slideshow. With just four mouse clicks you can set up the length of the show, the transition to be used between slides, and the motion effects to be used on each slide. To let Encore do the hard work for you:

1   If the Slideshow Options pane is hidden, click on the Hide/Show arrow at the right edge of the Slideshow viewer.

2   Select Fit Slideshow to Audio Duration. Encore will figure out how long to make each slide so that the display of the last slide ends at the same time as the audio. Encore uses the total time of all audio assets that are in the slideshow for its calculations.

3   Choose a transition from the Default Transition drop-down list in the Slideshow Options pane. This applies the selected transition to each slide change.

4   For motion effects, in the Slideshow Options pane of the Slideshow viewer, select Random Pan & Zoom. This option takes all of the available pan and zoom movements and applies them randomly to each slide.

Note: If you add transitions between slides and the audience navigates from slide to slide using the Next and Previous buttons on the DVD player's remote control, they will be taken to the beginning of the transition between the slides, not to the beginning of the next slide.

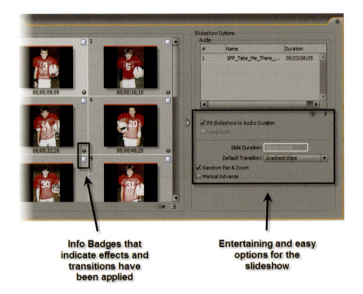

Info Badges that indicate effects and transitions have been applied

Entertaining and easy options for the slideshow

After you gain some experience making slideshows in Encore, you may feel that you need more control over individual slides, or that one or more of Encore's automatic settings are not appropriate. The tools available in the Slideshow Options pane and the Properties panel give you lots of options for making custom slideshows.

Note: By default, the Slide Duration control in the Slideshow Options pane of the Slideshow viewer sets all of the slides in the show to the same duration. To set the duration of a slide individually, use the Properties panel for that slide. Uncheck Match Slideshow in the Properties panel and then enter the desired duration.

Adding Subtitles to the Slideshow

With Adobe Encore DVD 2.0, you can easily add subtitles to a slideshow as captions to give your audience more information about the slides. Creating subtitles in the Slideshow viewer is somewhat different that creating subtitles in the Timeline viewer. Also unlike the Timeline viewer, you can't create the subtitles external to Encore and then import them; all subtitle text for a slideshow must be entered

Encore has extensive customization tools for slideshows

in your Encore project. Subtitles are added to slides using the Properties panel. To add subtitles to a slide:

1 In the Slideshow viewer, select a slide.

2 Select the Basic tab in the Properties panel.

3 Slideshow subtitles can be created with the name of the slide, a description of the slide, or both. Type the appropriate text in the Name and Description fields.

4 Check the Create Subtitle box and choose Name, Description or both.

5 Vertical placement of the subtitle is determined by the percentage value in the Alignment field. These values reference the top (0%) and bottom (100%) of the Title Safe Area, not the top and bottom of the whole slide. Choose a percentage value. The default is 100%.

6 All subtitles are aligned against the left edge of the Title Safe Area. Encore treats whatever is written in the Description field as a single paragraph with no hard returns. Subtitle text will wrap when it bumps up against the right edge of the Title Safe Area.

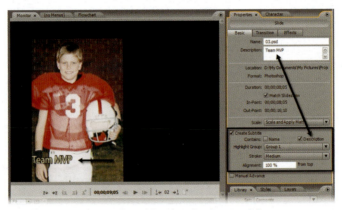

Options for adding a subtitle to a slide

Since a slideshow is a special kind of timeline, it has its own Timeline Color Set. Change the appearance of slideshow subtitle text the same way that the appearance of other subtitles in other timelines is changed. The procedure is outlined in the "Changing the Appearance of Subtitle Text" section of this chapter.

THE PROJECT:
Menu Design and Creation

Very much like their restaurant counterparts, the menus on a DVD provide the audience with a choice of selections that can be enjoyed as a whole or sampled à la carte. On more complex discs, they provide access to every part of a DVD, allowing the audience to construct a satisfying experience, from appetizers all the way through to dessert. But navigation isn't the whole story behind the menus in a DVD. Menus can be used to add interactive content and special effects, and their design is how the author really personalizes the DVD, giving it a certain look and feel. Menu design and creation is the heart and soul of your DVD project. It's that important.

In this chapter, we will discuss how to add menus and menu objects to the project, but we won't talk about how to set up those objects for disc navigation just yet. That will be covered in "The Project: Linking Everything Together".

Encore Menus As Photoshop Files

First and foremost, you need to understand that an Encore menu is a Photoshop file. It is important, therefore, to establish a basic knowledge of how Photoshop files work. If you are an experienced Photoshop user, this information will be familiar and mercifully brief. If you haven't worked with Photoshop files before, this primer focuses only on the essential features of a Photoshop file that make menu creation in Encore possible.

Every Photoshop file consists of at least one *layer*. A simple image like a scanned photograph will only have a background layer that contains the entire image. A more complex image is often constructed of two or several layers. For example, if you add a caption to your scanned photo, the text for the caption is on its own layer, above the background image.

The view of the image is seen from the top down, through all of the layers. Any part of any layer that is transparent will allow what lies below to show through.

While you are editing your menu inside of Encore, it works like a layered Photoshop image. Many of the menu objects are on their own layer; they can be stacked in any order. Changing the stacking order of menu objects is called *arranging* inside of Encore.

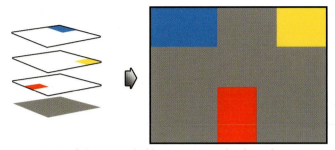

View of the expanded layers in a simple photoshop file and the resulting composited image

Each menu object can be moved around inside the frame of the menu without disturbing the position of the other objects. You can position multiple objects at the same time by selecting the layers you want to move and dragging them to where you want them. Multiple objects can be evenly spaced across all or part of the menu by using the *Align* and *Distribute* commands. We will talk more about these commands later on in the chapter.

The Menu Design Workspace

Designing menus requires that we have more panels immediately accessible than we needed for creating timelines and slideshows. To switch to the Menu Design workspace do either of the following:

1   Select Window ▶ Workspace ▶ Menu Design.

2   From the drop-down list on the Toolbar, select Menu Design.

Getting Started

The quickest way to create menus for your project is to start with a menu template from the Encore Library. With one of Encore's menus as a foundation, you can easily add, delete and rearrange objects to fit the scope of your project. The Encore Library includes a large collection of complete menus, for both Standard and Widescreen projects.

Note: The Educational and Tryout versions of Adobe Encore DVD 2.0 do not include as much Library content as the full Retail version. Videogears.com has

107

The Menu Design workspace

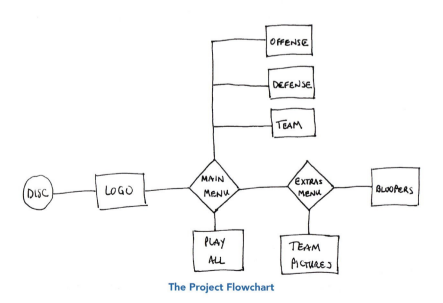

The Project Flowchart

some free and some inexpensive menu resources that can help you fill the content gap between these versions.

For our project, we will use a Standard menu template that is included in the Encore Library. The example flowchart from "The Project: Planning" will guide us as we modify and duplicate the template.

To create a menu using a template from the Library:

1   Select the Library panel.

2   Choose a Library Set from the drop-down list at the top of the panel.

The Library Set drop-down list and the Library panel filtered to show only menus

The New Menu button

3   Click on the Menu button at the top of the list area. This limits the display of items in the list to complete menus only.

4   Highlight a menu in the list and then click on the New Menu button at the bottom of the panel.

Note: Creating a menu for a Widescreen project is as simple as choosing a Widescreen menu template. Widescreen menu templates that shipped with Adobe Encore DVD 2.0 are indicated in the Library by the word "WIDE" in the name of the template.

When you create a new menu, it will automatically appear in the Menu viewer. The menu that is currently visible in the Menu viewer is called the *active* menu.

In Encore, there is almost always more than one way to accomplish a given task. You can also create a new menu using the Menu ▶ New Menu (Ctrl+M) command. However, this method will not create a new menu with the menu template that you select in the Library panel. Instead, it creates a new menu with the default menu template in the current Library Set. To set a menu as the default menu for its Library Set:

1   Choose a Library Set from the drop-down list at the top of the Library panel.

2   Right-click the menu template in the list that you want to be the new default menu and choose Set As Default Menu.

3   A star icon will be attached to the menu icon for the new default menu.

The default menu icon

Manipulating Menu Objects

Encore has three tools for selecting and moving menu objects. They each have distinct functions, and knowing the difference between each of the tools will aid you quite a bit as you work in the Menu viewer. As always, if you make a mistake, the Undo (Ctrl+Z) command will get things back to where they were. Here's what these three important tools do:

- The Selection Tool (V) – This tool selects menu buttons. It selects entire buttons and that's all it selects. Ever. It may be helpful to think of it as the "Button Tool". Your cursor changes to a pointer with an oval while you are working in the Menu viewer to indicate that this tool is active.

- The Direct Select Tool (A) – This is the most useful tool. It selects any layer of any object in the menu (including buttons!) as long as that layer isn't overlapped by another layer. In the Menu viewer, your cursor changes to an arrowhead when this tool is active.

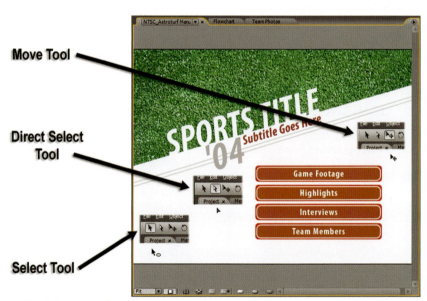

The Selection and Move Tools in the Toolbar and their icons in the Menu viewer

• The Move Tool (M) – This tool can't select anything. Its function is to move previously selected layers or objects from one place to another by clicking and dragging.

You can select menu objects and individual layers in the Menu viewer or in the Layers panel. Hold down the (Ctrl) key and click on multiple objects to make them part of the selection. Once selected, a menu object will be surrounded by a *bounding box*. The bounding box has tiny white squares, or *handles*, at each corner and at the midpoint of each side. Handles are used to resize and rotate the selected object. No matter which of the three tools is active, you can always resize, rotate and move the selected object. Here's how it works:

1   *Resize*: To resize the selected object, hover the cursor over one of the handles. The cursor will change to a double-headed arrow. Click and drag the handle to resize the object. Holding down the (Shift) key while you drag will scale the object without distortion. Holding down (Alt+Shift) while you drag will scale the object from the center without distortion.

2   *Rotate*: To rotate the selected object, hover the cursor over one of the handles, but just outside the limits of the bounding box. The cursor will change to a curved, double-headed arrow. Click and drag the handle to rotate the whole object around its center point. Holding down the (Shift) key *after* you start rotating will limit the rotation of the object to 45-degree increments.

3   *Move*: To move the selected object, hover the cursor over the interior area of the bounding box.

The selected object showing the bounding box, handles and handle cursor shapes

The cursor will not change shape, but if you click and drag, the selected object will move. Similar to rotating an object, holding down the (Shift) key *after* you start dragging will limit the movement of the object to a pure vertical, a pure horizontal or a pure 45-degree diagonal axis.

The Move tool is especially useful for moving objects and layers that are overlapped in the Menu viewer by other layers or objects. To use the Move tool:

1   In the Layers panel, select one or more layers that you want to move. Notice that a bounding box for each selected layer is now visible in the Menu viewer.

2   Select the Move tool (M).

3   Click and drag the selected layer(s) to move them to their new location.

The selected layers in the Layers panel and the Menu viewer

The Safe Area

You can toggle the display of the Safe Area on and off in the Menu viewer. The Safe Area shows both the Action Safe Area (the outer rectangle) and the Title Safe Area (the inner rectangle). As we work in Encore, we will be concerned exclusively with the Title Safe Area.

Having the Title Safe Area marked in the Menu viewer while you work is important if the finished DVD will be shown on a consumer television set. Because broadcast television programs have timing signals and other artifacts at the extreme edges of the frame, almost all TVs are *overscanned* to push these ugly

**Use this button to toggle the display
of the Safe Areas on and off**

artifacts out of the viewable area so that they are never seen by the audience. Even though a DVD isn't a broadcast program, it can still be affected by overscan. If you put your menu objects too close to the edge of the video frame while you are working on your computer, parts of them could get pushed off-screen when the menu is displayed on a TV. Keeping all of your menu objects inside the Title Safe Area ensures that they won't get cut off.

In addition to the Safe Area display, you can see how your menu will look on a TV if you enable Edit ▶ Preferences ▶ Audio/Video Out ▶ Show Menu Editor on DV Hardware. You will need to connect your computer's firewire port to a DV device, and hook up a monitor to the analog outputs of that device.

Note: The Safe Area display will not show up in the project Preview or the finished DVD, nor will it appear if you send the Menu viewer signal to an external monitor.

Replacing Text in Menu Objects

All of the Encore menu templates that are included in the Library have text placeholders as part of the design of the menu. These placeholders contain generic text that must be changed to fit your project. This is the first modification that we will make to our project menu. Use the Text tool to make the changes. To replace the text in the placeholders for buttons and graphics:

1 Select the Text tool (T) from the Toolbar.

2 Position your cursor over the text in the Menu viewer that you wish to replace. It will change to an I-beam.

3 Pay close attention to the shape of the cursor. If a solid outline of a square appears around a dotted I-beam, it means that you are not hovering over existing text. Move the cursor precisely over the existing text until the I-beam is solid and not surrounded by the outline.

4 Once the cursor shape is a solid I-beam without the outline, drag the cursor over the text you wish to replace.

5 Type in new text.

6 To exit the text-editing mode, press the (Esc) key or select a different tool.

The different text cursors

Duplicating Menus and Menu Objects

Our flowchart tells us that we need another menu to give the audience access to all of our program content. We could create a whole new menu from the template again, but since we've already modified our first menu, it is easier and faster to duplicate our modified menu and then make changes to that. You will

The original menu template and the text changes in the new menu

find this to be true in almost every project. To duplicate a menu:

1   In the Project panel, select the menu you want to duplicate.

2   Choose Edit ▶ Duplicate (Ctrl+D).

Now we've got two menus. One will be the Main Menu and the other will be the Extras Menu. According to our flowchart, that's all of the menus that we'll need. Let's look at the Main Menu first. We've customized it some by changing the text placeholders, but now we need to create a way to let the audience navigate to the Extras Menu.

When you want to add stuff to a menu and yet stay within the look and feel of the menu template, you can either add items from the Library that support the design of the template or you can duplicate existing menu objects and then modify those. We'll duplicate a text object to make a new menu button that will allow navigation to the Extras Menu.

To duplicate a menu object, select the object you want to duplicate in the Layers panel and do either of the following:

1   Choose Edit ▶ Duplicate (Ctrl+D).

2   Use the Move tool (M) while holding down the (Alt) key and drag the selected object to duplicate it.

The duplicated text object needs new text, and it is neither the right size nor in the right place. We'll fix that by replacing the text, moving the object and then resizing it.

The duplicated text object after (Alt+dragging) the
original text object

The modified Main Menu showing all of the modified text
placeholders

Converting a Text Object to a Button

A text object can be converted to a button. The text itself becomes the button; there is no need for other graphics. This technique is often used on multiple-menu DVDs where a link back to the main menu is provided on a sub-menu. For our project, we will create a text button to link from the Main Menu to the Extras Menu and vice-versa. To convert a text object to a button:

1 Select the text object in the Layers panel.

2 Click in the empty square just to the left of the text icon. This square is in the Object/Button column of the Layers panel; it is used to convert an object to a button.

3 A small, white rectangle appears in the square. The rectangle is called a button icon and it indicates that the layer is now a button.

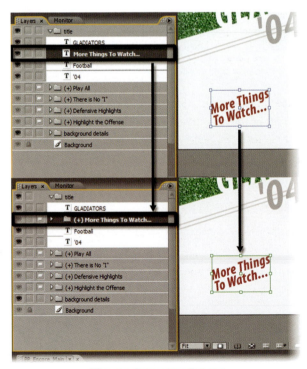

The text becomes a button

The button icon in the Object/Button column of the Layers panel isn't the only indication that an object is a button. Encore knows which menu objects are buttons by the way that they are named in the Layers panel. In Photoshop-speak, an Encore menu button is a *layer set* – a group of two or more layers that act as a single object. Encore recognizes a layer set as a button only if the layer set has the correct *prefix* as part of its name. The prefix (+) indicates a button layer set.

A menu button layer set in the Layers panel

The text we duplicated was part of a layer set called "title". When we converted it into a button, that button became part of the same layer set. To keep the organization of the menu layers logical, we should move the text button's layer setup higher in the stacking order, to the same level as the other buttons in the menu. To arrange objects in the Layers panel:

1 Choose Object ▶ Arrange.

2 Select Bring Forward (Ctrl+]) to move the layer up higher in the stacking order. Select Send Backward (Ctrl+[) to move the layer lower in the stacking order. These commands move the selected layer up or down one layer at a time.

3 Select Bring to Front (Shift+Ctrl+]) to move the selected layer immediately to the top of the Layers panel. Select Send to Back (Shift+Ctrl+[) to move the layer down below all other layers except the background layer. Nothing can be below the background.

**The new button's layer set has been moved higher
up in the Layers panel**

Note: If a layer set is expanded in the Layers panel when the Bring Forward or Send Backward commands are applied, the selected layer can move into or out of the expanded layer set. If a layer set is collapsed in the Layers panel, those commands will cause the selected layer to skip over the layer set.

Now that our new button is in place, both in the menu's layout and in the Layers panel, we need to give it a subpicture highlight:

1 Select the new button in the Layers panel or in the Menu viewer.

2 In the Properties panel, select the Create Text Subpicture checkbox.

I can almost hear the question forming in your mind: "What in the world is a subpicture highlight?" Relax. We're going to discuss that next.

The Subpicture Highlight

If you expand a button layer set in the Layers panel, you can see the individual layers that make up the button. Within a button layer set is a special layer called

Give the new text button a subpicture highlight

the *subpicture layer*. The prefixes (=1), (=2) and (=3) are used to indicate a subpicture layer. For our project menus, we will only be concerned with the (=1) prefix. Adobe Encore DVD 2.0 uses the subpicture layer in a button layer set, together with the Menu Color Set, to generate the *subpicture highlight* for the button. On the finished DVD, subpicture highlights give visual feedback to the audience when they use the navigation keys on the DVD player's remote control to move from button to button on a menu. This visual feedback involves a color and/or a transparency change that distinguishes the selected button from the other menu buttons.

Let me emphasize a distinction here that is very important to understanding the concept of subpicture highlights in Encore. The *subpicture layer* in an Encore button layer set is the basis for the *subpicture highlight* that the audience sees when they navigate to that button. Encore takes the subpicture layer, and following the instructions in the Menu Color Set, generates the subpicture highlight. We'll talk about the Menu Color Set in a moment.

Note: Not every menu button has to have a subpicture layer. Our text button doesn't have one because Encore generates the subpicture highlight automatically from the text itself. If a DVD author wants to hide a menu button from the audience as part of a special feature called an *Easter Egg,* that button might not contain a subpicture layer, either, because a subpicture highlight would give away the location of the hidden button.

The layers that make up a button layer set. Notice the prefix on the subpicture layer

When a DVD disc is played back, the subpicture highlight for each button on a menu is always displayed in one of three *states*: Normal, Selected or Activated. A button's subpicture highlight is never just "off"; it must always be displayed in one of the three states. Normal is the button's unselected state. The Selected state is used when the audience has navigated to that button using the directional arrow keys on the DVD player's remote control. The Activated state for a button is triggered by pushing the Enter button on the remote control.

Note: There are other ways to get a menu button into the Selected or Activated states, but we will discuss those in "The Project: Linking Everything Together".

It is useful to think of the subpicture highlight as an *overlay*; on the finished DVD it is displayed on top of all the other menu layers. When Encore builds the project for burning to DVD, all of the graphic, text and video menu objects except the button subpicture highlights are flattened into a single video layer. The subpicture highlights are displayed over this video layer. The subpicture highlight for each button is only visible within a rectangle that closely surrounds the button. The rest of the subpicture layer is transparent. It is this transparency in the subpicture layer that allows us to see the menu layers underneath it.

Now let's look at the text button we created earlier. We need to view the Selected state of its subpicture highlight. To change which subpicture highlight state you are seeing in the Menu viewer, click on one of the Show Subpicture Highlight buttons at the bottom of the viewer. The Menu viewer shows that state for all of the menu's buttons simultaneously.

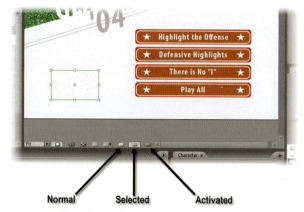

Normal   Selected   Activated

The Show Subpicture Highlight buttons

Notice that in the Selected state, the subpicture highlight for the text button looks pretty bad. It has rough, jagged edges and doesn't blend well at all with the text underneath. We will correct those problems by making changes to the Menu Color Set.

The Menu Color Set

Similar to the way that the appearance of subtitles is changed using the Timeline Color Set, subpicture highlight appearance is changed by modifying the Menu Color Set. When you modify a menu's color set, you change the instructions that tell Encore how to generate subpicture highlights from the subpicture layers in the menu's button layer sets. The subpicture layers themselves are not changed at all.

Encore always includes a Menu Default color set when you start a new project. The Menu Default color set is a single color set that is available to all menus in the project, and it will be the same for every new project that you start. Encore also generates an Automatic color set when you import or create a menu. The Automatic color set is based on the colors of the objects in the menu. That's very cool. Each menu has its own distinct Automatic color set.

The Automatic color set that Encore generates for a menu cannot be changed. You can, however, create a new, modifiable color set that is based on the

Automatic color set. Here's how:

1 With the Menu viewer forward, choose Menu ▶ Edit Menu Color Set.

2 Make sure the Automatic color set is displayed in the Color Set drop-down list and then click on the New Color Set button.

3 Give the new color set a name like Modified Automatic. The colors in the new set are identical to the colors in the Automatic set, only now they can be modified.

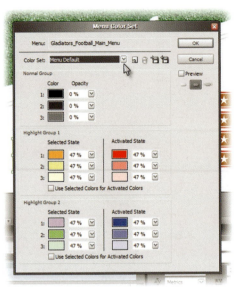

The Menu Default color set. This color set is available to all menus in a project

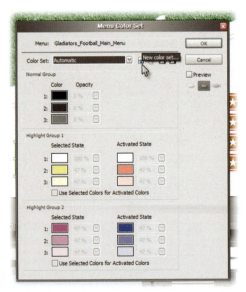

The Automatic color set for a menu, and the New Color Set button. Note that this color set cannot be modified

The Menu Color Set dialog is divided into three groups: Normal, Highlight Group 1 and Highlight Group 2. Let's look at the Normal Group first. The Normal Group settings tell Encore how the subpicture highlight should look for menu buttons that aren't selected or activated. In other words, the Normal Group controls the Normal subpicture highlight state. In most cases, the DVD author won't want any visible highlights for this state. But the subpicture highlight is never off and must always be

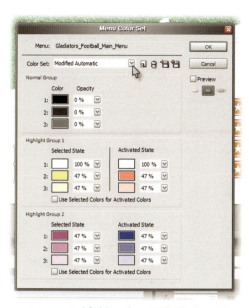

A new, modifiable color set that is based on the Automatic color set

displayed, so any color used in the Normal Group will always be seen over unselected buttons. How do we keep the subpicture highlight from appearing on top of buttons that are in the Normal state? The answer is that we change the transparency of the highlight. Remember that Encore and other Adobe applications use opacity to control transparency; 0% opaque is the same thing as 100% transparent. Notice that in our project menu, the opacity values for the Normal

Group colors are set to 0%. Those colors are completely transparent and won't be seen by the audience when a menu button is in the Normal state.

At first glance, it appears that Highlight Group 1 and Highlight Group 2 might correspond to the other subpicture highlight states – Selected and Activated. But that's not the case. Highlight Group 1 and Highlight Group 2 are completely independent sets of controls; only one of them is

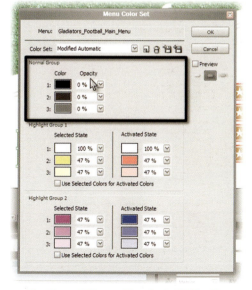

The Normal Group. Opacity is 0% for the Normal Group colors

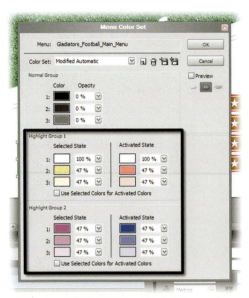

Highlight Groups 1 and 2

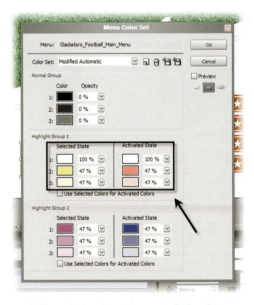

The color and opacity controls for the Selected and Activated states

required to tell Encore how to generate the Selected and Activated states of the menu's subpicture highlights. All menu buttons default to using Highlight Group 1. The purpose of having a second highlight group is to give the DVD author the flexibility to have different subpicture highlights for different groups of menu buttons. One highlight group might control the subpicture highlights for the menu buttons that take the audience to the program content, and the other highlight group would control the highlights for the buttons that take the audience to other menus. There is an example of this in the Advanced Design Techniques section of "The Project: Linking Everything Together". In a moment, we'll use the two sets of Highlight Group controls to fix the subpicture highlight for our text button without changing the subpicture highlights for the other menu buttons.

There is another question about the Menu Color Set dialog that needs to be answered: why do the highlight groups have three colors for each state? The answer is straightforward: it's because the subpicture highlight can have up to three colors for each state. However, each of the highlight colors has to have its own subpicture layer in the Layers panel. Remember the three different prefixes that can indicate a subpicture layer? The color and opacity of the subpicture highlight for the (=1) subpicture layer is determined by the color and opacity settings for number 1 in the Menu Color Set dialog, the color and opacity of the highlight for the (=2) subpicture layer is determined by the color and opacity settings for number 2, and likewise for the (=3) subpicture layer. Realistically, you can only take full advantage of the (=2) and (=3) subpicture layers if you create your menus inside of Adobe Photoshop, so we will discuss how best to use this feature in the chapter, "Interacting with Other Adobe Software".

Changing the Appearance of Subpicture Highlights

Let's fix that ugly subpicture highlight for our text button now. We're going to use Highlight Group 2 to control the subpicture for the button. Here's what we have to do:

1 Make sure that a color set other than Automatic is selected in the Menu Color Set dialog and click OK. For our example we will use the Modified Automatic color set.

2 Select the text button in the Menu viewer.

3 In the Properties panel, click on the drop-down arrow in the Highlight control and choose Group 2.

4 Open the Menu Color Set dialog again by choosing Menu ▶ Edit Menu Color Set. Position the dialog so that you can see the button to be modified in the Menu viewer.

5 In the Highlight Group 2 control set, click on the color swatch for number 1 under Selected State and choose a white color in the Color Picker dialog. It doesn't have to be pure white; a grayish-white will do fine.

6 Set the opacity for number 1 to a value that is about halfway transparent. You cannot type in your own percentage. There are only 16 levels of opacity available for each highlight color, and all 16 are listed in the drop-down box. In this case 47% works nicely.

7   Keeping the look and feel of our menu template means that the Activated state of our text button needs to be the same as the Selected State. Take care of this little detail quickly by checking the Use Selected Colors for Activated Colors box.

8   Check the Preview box under the Cancel button and then click the Show Selected Subpicture Highlight button. Back in the Menu viewer, our text button now has a nice, soft subpicture highlight for the Selected state. Click OK to save the changes to the color set.

The modified Menu Color Set

Also in the Menu viewer, notice that the subpicture highlights for the other menu buttons haven't changed. That's because they are still using Highlight Group 1 colors, and we modified Highlight Group 2. We will make the same changes to the Extras Menu.

A Special Effect Using Subpicture Highlights

We can use the Menu Color Set to create a popular menu special effect: images that are part of a button layer set appear to be monochrome in the

The Selected state of all the menu buttons

Normal state, and they pop into full color when the button is selected. Here's how to do it:

1 Start with a menu that has full-color images for its buttons, or as part of its button layer set.

2 Open the Menu Color Set dialog. Adjust its position so that you can see the buttons in the Menu viewer. Click on the New Color Set button and create a new color set.

3 In the Normal Group, change the appropriate color swatch to a neutral gray. For example, if the subpicture layer for the button has (=1) as a prefix, then change the number 1 color swatch to R = 128, G = 128 and B = 128.

4 Adjust the opacity of the neutral gray highlight color to a value that washes out the color in the image, yet doesn't completely hide the details. Opacity values between 73% and 93% generally work well for this. If the image has areas of very strong, bright colors, then you won't be able to get a true monochrome effect without completely obscuring the image.

5   In Highlight Group 1, change the opacity of the appropriate highlight color to 0%. As above, if the subpicture layer has the prefix (=1), then change the opacity of the number 1 highlight color. Since you are making the color transparent, it doesn't matter what the color of the swatch is.

6   Click OK to save changes to the Menu Color Set.

When the menu buttons are in the Normal state, they will be covered with the monochrome highlight overlay. When a button is selected, the highlight becomes transparent and the button appears to pop into full color.

The menu buttons appear to pop into full color when they are selected

Aligning and Distributing Menu Objects

As you add, delete and move menu objects around, the layout for the menu changes. For example, let's say you added several buttons so that viewers could select different chapters of the program and you want to align and distribute those buttons evenly across the menu. Dragging each one to the vicinity of its desired location and then painstakingly trying to line them up is tedious and frustrating work. Adobe Encore DVD 2.0 provides you with the tools you need to do this kind of arranging quickly and with a minimum of fuss.

Align

The Align commands are used to line up multiple objects. They don't space out the selected objects evenly, they just line them up. It is usually a good idea to use these commands together with the Distribute commands.

The alignment is done relative to either of two boxes. The first box is the Title Safe Area. The second box is a bounding box that contains all of the selected objects. Encore calculates this imaginary bounding box around the objects and alignment occurs completely inside of the box.

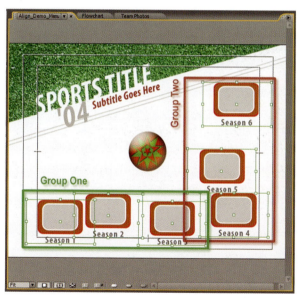

Two groups of menu buttons and their imaginary bounding boxes before alignment

The Title Safe Area is a good choice because it represents the practical upper limit of available space in which to spread out your objects. Even though you could use more of the space near the edges of the frame than the Title Safe

THE FOCAL EASY GUIDE TO ADOBE® ENCORE™ DVD 2.0

Area allows, you don't want to put any menu objects closer to the edges than that; remember that they may get cut off by overscan when displayed on a TV set. To align multiple objects relative to the Title Safe Area:

1 Select the objects you want to align.

2 Choose Object ▶ Align ▶ Relative to Safe Areas. This option will remain checked and all future alignment commands will be performed relative to the Title Safe Area.

3 Choose Object ▶ Align again. There is a chance for some confusion as you make your next selection, so let's look at the choices carefully.

4 If the objects you want to line up are arranged vertically, that is they are spread out across the menu roughly from top-to-bottom, you need to select from the Left/Center/Right alignment group. Select Left to line up the left edges of the objects with the left edge of the Title Safe Area; Center to line up the centers of the objects with the center of the Title Safe Area; or Right to line up the right edges of the objects with the right edge of the Title Safe Area.

5 If the objects you want to line up are arranged horizontally, that is they are spread out across the menu more or less from side-to-side, you need to select from the Top/Middle/Bottom alignment group. Select Top to line up the tops of the objects with the top of the Title Safe Area; Middle to line up the centers of the objects with the center of the Title Safe Area; or Bottom to line up the bottoms of the objects with the bottom of the Title Safe Area.

Note: It seems to go against logic that you would use vertical alignment commands for horizontally arranged objects, and vice-versa, but that's how it works. If you used the horizontal alignment commands on horizontally arranged objects, they would all end up on top of each other.

To tell Encore to use the imaginary bounding box as the reference for object alignment, select Object ▶ Align and make sure the Relative to Safe Areas option is unchecked. All Align command choices are made the same way as before, only this time Encore will align the objects relative to the imaginary bounding box instead of the Title Safe Area.

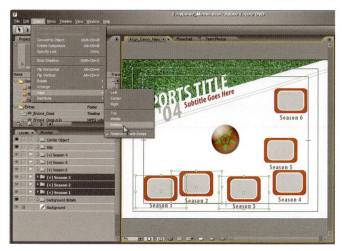

Ready to Align the Group One buttons with the bottom of the Title Safe Area

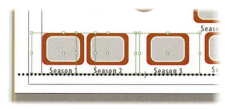

The Group One buttons after aligning them to the bottom of the Title Safe Area

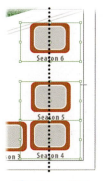

Notice that even after lining up the buttons, they are not evenly spaced out. The Align commands line up the buttons but they do nothing to fix the spacing between them. That's where the Distribute commands come in handy.

The Group Two buttons after aligning them to the center of the imaginary bounding box

Distribute

The Distribute commands are used to evenly space out multiple objects. They don't line up the objects that are being spaced out, so again, it is usually a good idea to use them together with the Align commands.

There are only two choices for the direction of distribution: Vertically and Horizontally. There are no imaginary boxes to be calculated using these commands; all movement is referenced to either the Title Safe Area or to the objects themselves. Encore looks for the two outermost objects in the chosen direction and calculates the distribution between them. If you choose to distribute the objects relative to the Title Safe Area, the outermost objects will be placed against the edges of the Title Safe Area.

Note: Unless more than two objects are selected when you try to use the Distribute command with Relative to Safe Areas unchecked, the Vertically and Horizontally choices will be disabled. It doesn't make sense to tell Encore to distribute only two objects relative to each other because they are already distributed no matter where they are! If thinking about that makes your head hurt, don't worry. The important thing is that if the Distribute command choices are unavailable, you just need to select more objects or tell Encore to reference the Title Safe Area.

To distribute multiple objects:

1   Select the objects that you want to be distributed evenly.

2   Choose Object ▶ Distribute. Check or uncheck Relative to Safe Areas depending on whether you want to distribute the objects relative to the Title Safe Area or not. Your choice will remain in effect until you change it again.

3   Choose Object ▶ Distribute again.

4   Select Vertically if you want the objects to be distributed evenly from top-to-bottom.

5   Select Horizontally if you want the objects to be distributed evenly from left-to-right.

Note: If you are thinking at this point that, even though the buttons are now lined up and evenly spaced, the overall menu layout doesn't look very good, then I agree. This menu and final button arrangement were chosen to illustrate

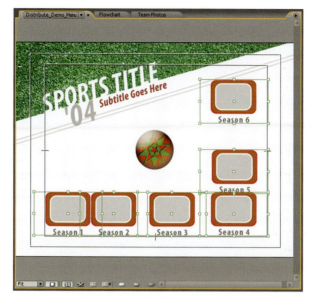

**The two selected menu button groups after using the
Align command and before using the Distribute command**

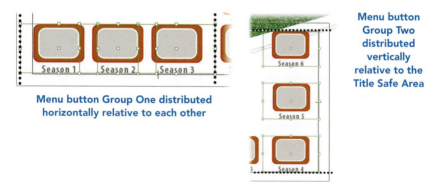

**Menu button Group One distributed
horizontally relative to each other**

**Menu button
Group Two
distributed
vertically
relative to the
Title Safe Area**

the Align and Distribute commands, not to show off my design skills or to integrate into our project.

Button Routing

Once the menu buttons are where you want them, it is time to decide how to *route* them. Button routing defines which button on a menu will be selected next when the audience pushes one of the directional arrow keys on the DVD player's remote control. When one of the arrow keys is pressed, the DVD player wants to know two things:

- What button am I on now?

- What button do I go to next?

In Adobe Encore DVD 2.0, these two questions are answered by the menu's button numbers. Every button on a menu has a number. Encore automatically assigns button numbers and their routing when a new menu is created. And, because Encore is designed to make things as easy for you as possible, Encore automatically updates the button numbers and the routing if you add or delete buttons, or if you change the menu layout by using the Align and Distribute commands.

Note: You can change the logic that Encore uses to automatically route buttons by changing the options under Edit ▶ Preferences ▶ Menu.

Very often, the default or automatically updated routing will work just fine. But in some cases, Encore's routing choices may not make sense in a modified design layout. You can expose Encore's button routing and easily make changes so that your audience can navigate from button to button without confusion. To show the current button routing and make changes to it:

1 Click on the Show Button Routing button in the Menu viewer. You will see a routing icon that looks like a black cross for each button. There will be a button number in the center of the icon and a number in each of the four arms of the icon. If a routing icon is green, it means that button is currently selected.

2 In the Project panel, select the menu that is active in the Menu viewer. This brings up the menu's properties in the Properties panel.

3 In the Properties panel, uncheck Automatically Route Buttons. This is a critical step because you can't change Encore's automatic button routing while this option is selected.

4 Back in the Menu viewer, position your cursor over the routing icon of a button whose routing you want to change. The center number is the button's number. The numbers in the arms of the icon indicate the button that will be selected next when the audience presses that directional arrow key on the DVD player's remote.

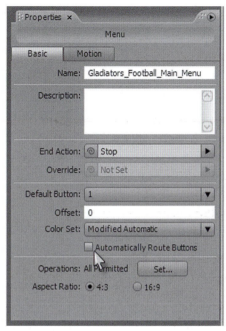

5 Move the cursor over the arm of the icon that corresponds to the routing destination that you want to change. The cursor will change to a hand icon. Click and drag the hand to the new destination button.

Uncheck Automatically Route Buttons when you want to change a menu's button routing

6 To disable any of the four routing destinations for a button, you have to route the button to itself in that direction. To route a button to itself, drag the hand outside of the button's bounding box and then back in again.

7 Repeat until all buttons are routed the way you want in all directions.

Note: The bounding boxes around the buttons when Show Button Routing is active indicate the space required for each of the buttons as seen by a DVD player. It is also the area within which the button's subpicture highlight is displayed. If any of these bounding boxes overlap, then button navigation on a DVD player will get messed up. Adjust the alignment and distribution of your buttons so that their bounding boxes never overlap when the Menu viewer is set to Show Button Routing.

The menu buttons and their routing icons when Show
Button Routing is active in the Menu viewer. Notice the
hand icon and the button bounding boxes

Building Your Own Menu

Building a menu from scratch takes more thought and preparation than using a
menu template from the Library, but it offers the chance to create menus that fit
your artistic vision for the finished DVD that cannot be matched by any pre-
designed template.

You can use almost any graphics program with which you are comfortable to
create custom graphics and backgrounds that will work directly in Encore.
Background audio and video can also be imported into Encore and used as part
of the menu.

Note: In the following sections I will talk about creating menus on a generic
level. If you are an Adobe Photoshop user, you have virtually unlimited capability
at your disposal to create and customize your menus for Encore. Using Adobe
Photoshop for menu design and creation will be discussed in the chapter,
"Interacting With Other Adobe Software".

Static Menu Backgrounds

A static menu background uses an image or graphic that is big enough to fill the entire frame of DVD video. Text, buttons and other graphics will be placed on top of this background layer. How big does a graphic need to be in order to be used as a menu background? Well, in the NTSC television system, a Standard frame of DVD video is 720 pixels wide by 480 pixels high. So that's how big we need to make our Standard NTSC background graphics, right? Well, maybe. Let's talk about that.

It is important to note that Standard NTSC DVD video pixels are not square. They are taller than they are wide. The measure of how wide a pixel is, compared to its height, is known as Pixel Aspect Ratio, or PAR. So NTSC DVD video is really 720 pixels wide by 480 pixels high with a PAR of 0.9.

When you design your background graphics on a computer, you will be designing them while watching what you're doing on a monitor. Computer monitors display square pixels. Conveniently, all computer graphics programs work with square pixels. But that doesn't help us much with our rectangular DVD video pixels, does it? Some graphics programs understand rectangular pixels, but the majority of them do not. If your graphics program only supports square pixels (e.g. any version of Photoshop prior to Photoshop CS) then you will need to take this PAR stuff into account when you create your menu backgrounds. Otherwise, round circles won't appear round anymore. They will look like squished ovals. We could calculate the size of square-pixel graphics that will work in different types of DVD projects, but let's not. Instead, here's a list of the sizes you will need:

- Standard NTSC DVD:
  720 w × 534 h.

- Widescreen NTSC DVD:
  864 w × 480 h.

- Standard PAL DVD:
  768 w × 576 h.

- Widescreen PAL DVD:
  1024 w × 576 h.

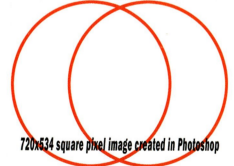

720x534 square pixel image created in Photoshop

A 720×534 square-pixel graphic as it would be displayed on TV by a DVD player. Notice the nice, round circles

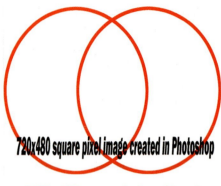

A 720×480 square-pixel graphic as it would be displayed on a TV by a DVD player. Notice how the round circles end up as squished ovals

Adobe Photoshop CS and Adobe Photoshop CS2 understand and can create rectangular pixel graphics. If you will be creating your menu graphics inside of either of these programs, then all you have to do to get perfectly sized menu backgrounds is to choose an image size preset in Photoshop that matches your DVD project.

Creating Menus from Backgrounds

Adobe Encore DVD 2.0 is very smart about scaling the images and graphics that are used in a project, making them just the right size for their intended purpose. However, a lot of Encore's scaling decisions are based on the rectangular pixel graphics that are used in its menu templates and that can be imported from Photoshop CS or Photoshop CS2. This may cause unexpected results if you import your square-pixel graphics as assets and then try to add them to a menu as a background.

We need a method that works in all cases, whether the background graphic is square-pixel, rectangular-pixel, Standard or Widescreen. The way to import graphics that will be used as menu backgrounds is to import them as menus and not as assets. Recall from "The Project: Importing Assets" that you import a file as a menu by selecting File ▶ Import As ▶ Menu (Shift+Ctrl+I).

Note: Since an Encore menu is a Photoshop file, Encore will only accept .psd files as menus or menu backgrounds. Many graphics programs have the ability to export a .psd file, so you should be able to meet this requirement easily.

Using the Library

We've already seen that importing a menu's background image as a menu is better than importing it as an asset and then trying to add it to a menu as the background. Similar logic applies to the graphics that will become part of the menu's buttons and design elements. Just as Encore's scaling decisions can cause problems for menu backgrounds, the problem for other graphics is that Encore ignores any transparency in the image if they are imported as assets. So rather than importing them as assets and adding them to a menu from the Project panel, it is better to add them to Encore's Library and then add them to the menu from there. This applies to any graphic format created in any graphics program, including Photoshop. A further advantage of using the Library is that the graphics are then available for use in other Encore projects.

Unlike menus and menu backgrounds, Encore will accept several graphics file formats for import into the Library; there is no requirement for your buttons or graphic design elements to be Photoshop files. To add graphics to the Library:

1   Select an existing Library Set or create a new one by opening the flyout menu and choosing New Set.

2   Click on the Image button at the top of the list area.

3   Click on the New Item button at the bottom of the panel.

4   Navigate to the location of your graphics, select one or more and then click OK.

5   The graphics are now part of the Library.

Adding graphics to the Library

Once the graphics are in the Library, it's easy to add them to a menu:

1   Select a Library Set from the Set drop-down list.

2   Click on the Image button at the top of the list area.

3   Select the object from the list that
    you want to add to the menu.

4   Click the Place button at the
    bottom of the Library panel to add
    the object to the active menu.

Creating Menu Buttons

The only way to create a layer set and
identify it as a button before it is added to
Encore's library is to use Adobe
Photoshop (version 6 or newer). If you
don't use Photoshop to create your
button graphics, you will have to convert
the graphics into buttons after you add
them to a menu. To turn button graphics
into actual menu buttons:

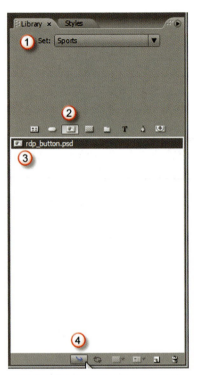

Adding the new graphic to a menu

1   Select the graphic in the Layers
    panel.

2   Click on the empty square to the
    left of the layer name, in the
    Object/Button column of the Layers panel.

3   A button icon appears. The layer has been converted from a single
    graphic to a layer set and the layer name now has a proper button prefix
    in front of it.

When a button is created this way, Encore automatically adds a subpicture
layer for the button's subpicture highlight. If the highlight doesn't look the way
you want or expect, you can modify its appearance using the techniques we
discussed earlier in this chapter.

If you exported the button graphic from your graphics program as a Photoshop
file, then any layers that are part of the button in your graphics program will
show up in Encore as separate layers in the Layers panel. Choose which of the

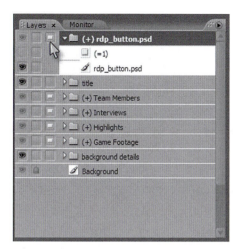

The new button. Notice the indicator in the Object/Button Column of the Layers panel, the new layer set icon and the new button name including the proper prefix

button layers you want to convert to a button carefully, because Encore will create a subpicture layer for the whole button's subpicture highlight from the layer that you choose. Once you have converted a layer into a button, use the Object ▶ Arrange commands to bring the rest of the button layers into the new button layer set, making sure the new subpicture layer is the topmost layer in the set. This preservation of the layer structure in the .psd file from your graphics program gives you much more creative flexibility inside of Encore to determine how you want your finished buttons and highlights to look.

Creating an Entire Menu External to Encore

If you create a complete, layered menu in your graphics program, it is possible to import the entire menu into Encore at once instead of adding the button graphics separately to an imported menu background. Remember that Encore requires that your menu be saved as a Photoshop file from your graphics program. Just as with button graphics that are saved as .psd files, any layers that are part of the structure of the menus in your graphics program will be brought into Encore as separate layers. To add a complete menu to your Encore project and convert button graphics to menu buttons:

1   Import the saved .psd file as a menu in the Project panel via File ▶ Import As ▶ Menu (Shift+Ctrl+I).

2   Pick one of the layers that make up a button graphic and convert that layer to a button. Choose carefully – Encore will create a subpicture layer for the whole button's subpicture highlight from this layer.

3 Use the Object ▶ Arrange commands to move the rest of the layers for that button graphic into the new button layer set. Make sure that the subpicture layer is the topmost layer in the button layer set.

4 Repeat steps 2 and 3 for each button graphic in the menu.

Adding a Text Object to a Menu

The only menu objects that can be created completely from scratch inside of Adobe Encore DVD 2.0 are text objects. Text objects are useful for design elements, buttons, captions and other information for the audience. To add a new text object:

1 Select the Text tool (T) from the toolbar.

2 Position the cursor over the menu where you want the text to start. Make sure there is a solid box around a dotted I-beam cursor to confirm that you aren't trying to modify existing text.

3 Drag the cursor to create a bounding box into which you can type your text.

4 Begin typing the new text. Text will wrap automatically.

If you select the text tool and click in the Menu viewer instead of clicking and dragging, you will create a free-form text object where the text will not wrap on its own. You will have to add hard returns with the (Enter) key to get the text to move to the next line.

You can use the Vertical Text tool (Y) to create a text object that is oriented vertically. The text characters will be turned 90 degrees to the right, so that it appears the left margin is toward the top of the screen. To give the appearance that the letters in the text object are stacked right-side up, one on top of the other, open the wing menu of the Character panel and choose Rotate Character.

Typing in a text bounding box

Free-form typing

A text object created with the Vertical Text tool (Y). Compare to a
text object whose characters have been rotated

145

Sometimes it is easier to read text against a background if you add a drop shadow. To quickly add a drop shadow to your text object:

1 Select the text object in the Menu viewer or the Layers panel.

2 Select Object ▶ Drop Shadow.

3 Adjust the color, position and size as desired from the Drop Shadow dialog box.

The Drop Shadow dialog

More shadow and glow effects for text are available from the Styles panel. To access these additional effects:

1 Select the Basic Style Set from the Set drop-down list.

2 Select the Text button to limit the display of effects to text styles only.

3 Select the style you want to apply and click the Apply Style button.

The Character Panel

Adobe Encore DVD 2.0 has powerful font formatting features built-in to the Character panel. In fact, there are more ways to change a font's appearance inside of Encore than there are in the word-processing software that was used to write this book!

The Styles panel displaying shadow and glow effects for text

We'll take a quick look at some of the formatting options that are available and what effect they have on text:

- *The Font Family List*: This is a list of font families on your system that are available to Encore. Unfortunately, there is no way to browse through the fonts in Encore to see how they look. You have to select them one at a time to find out how a text object looks with different fonts.

- *The Font Style List*: Within each font family there are various styles, such as regular, bold, italic, etc.

- *Font Size*: Select a size for the font. You can choose one of the presets from the list or type in an exact size. How exact? You can specify the size in decimal fractions if you want! Resizing text objects in the Menu viewer will change the size here, too.

- *Leading*: It's pronounced like the heavy metal that shields you from X-rays. What it does is adjust the space between lines of text as measured from the bottom of the text, or *baseline*. Auto sets the leading to the size of the font, plus 20%.

- *Kerning*: Adjusts the spacing between two adjacent characters. Select the text tool and click in the text object to place the insertion point between the two characters you want to adjust. Change the kerning value as desired. Adjusting the kerning value does not affect any other characters in the selected text object, nor does it affect any characters in any new or existing text objects. Selecting *Metrics* uses the font's original kerning values.

- *Tracking*: Super-kerning. It adjusts the space between all of the characters in the selected text. It also affects any new text objects.

- *Horizontal and Vertical Scale*: Expands or contracts the text in either the horizontal or vertical dimension.

- *Baseline Shift:* Takes the selected characters and moves them up or down relative to the baseline of the text.

Note: The Character panel font attributes always reference the baseline of the text. It doesn't matter if the text is oriented horizontally or vertically in the menu, changes are always made relative to the text's baseline.

- *Color*: Changes the color of the selected text. Click on the color swatch to bring up the Color Picker dialog. Adjust the slider in the color range spectrum and then click the desired color in the color field. If you know the exact color values of the color you want, in either HSB or RGB, then you can enter those values in the appropriate fields.

- *Font Style Buttons*: Apply special styles to the selected text. If your font family doesn't have a bold or italic style, then you can apply the Faux Bold or Faux Italic styles to simulate them. Be careful about leaving these styles selected when you create new text objects or you may get unintended and puzzling results. Click on the style button again to deselect it.

- *Alignment Options*: These options determine how the text will be aligned when it wraps or when a hard return is added. Align Left is the default, even if no alignment options are selected.

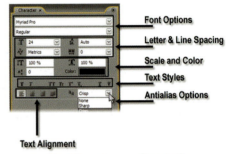

The Character panel controls

- *Text Antialias Mode*: Use this control to set how much you want the jagged edges of text to be smoothed. More smoothing results in a softer look to the text, and less smoothing gives the text a sharper, but a more jagged appearance.

Resizing Text Objects

Sometimes text isn't in the right place or doesn't flow across the menu the way you want. Or it may flow correctly and be in the right place, but needs to be larger or smaller.

There are two kinds of text resizing: scaling and reflow. Scaling text changes the size of the text object itself, with the result that the text inside is made larger or smaller and can be distorted in one direction or another. Reflow resizing changes the area that is occupied by the text, but the text itself is left unchanged.

To resize a text object using scaling:

1   Choose the Direct Select tool (A) and select the text object, either in the Menu viewer or the Layers panel.

2   Drag one of the handles just like you would for any other menu object.

3   If you don't want to distort the text during resizing, hold down the (Shift) or (Alt+Shift) keys while you drag to resize the text object proportionally without distortion.

To resize a text object using reflow:

1   Make sure the Text tool (T) is selected.

2   Click anywhere within the text object to activate the text's bounding box. Note that the handles of the bounding box are black, which indicates that reflow resizing is available. If you click on the text object and no bounding box appears, then the text object was created as a free-form text object and it cannot be reflow resized.

3   With the Text tool still active, drag one of the handles to resize the bounding box. Note that the (Shift) and (Alt+Shift) keyboard shortcuts have no effect when reflow resizing.

4   Watch the text reflow inside of the bounding box.

If you resize the bounding box to an area that is smaller than the area that is required by the text, the text will seem to disappear behind the edges of the bounding box. Don't worry. Your text hasn't really disappeared; it's still there. You just have to resize the bounding box again and make it large enough to expose all the text.

When you are finished editing text, press the (Esc) key to exit the editing mode. The text object can now be moved around the menu just like any other object.

Adding Style Effects

As with text, you can add Styles to menu objects. Often these Styles can give your menu objects depth and texture quickly and with significantly less effort than would be required to create the effect in a graphics program. To add Styles

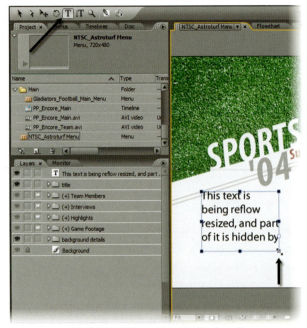

Reflow resizing using the Text tool

to your menu objects:

1   Select the object you want to modify in the Menu viewer or the Layers panel.

2   Bring the Styles panel forward in its frame.

3   Select a style set from the drop-down list.

4   Highlight a Style and click the Apply Style button at the bottom of the panel.

Adding Background Audio to a Menu

To add interest to your menus while the audience decides which program choice to make, you can add background audio to any menu. Here's how:

1   In the Project panel, select the menu to which you want to add background audio.

**The ZigZag Novelty Style applied to the Game Footage
button in the NTSC AstroTurf Menu template**

2 Select the tab for the Properties panel to bring it forward in its frame.

3 Select the Motion tab in the Properties panel.

4 In the Audio control, drag the pickwhip to an audio asset that is visible in the Project panel. The pickwhip is the little swirl icon in the Audio control. The target audio asset will be outlined in gray as the pickwhip passes over it.

5 The name of the target asset will be added to the Audio control, and the length of the asset will be shown in the Duration control. If you only want part of the asset to play as background audio, you can manually enter the duration. The timecode displayed in the Duration control is in the same HH;MM;SS;FF format as the timecode in the Timeline viewer and the Monitor panel.

Dragging the pickwhip into the Project panel

6   From the drop-down list in the
     Loop # control, select how many
     times you want the audio to
     loop before it stops. If you want
     the audio to continue looping until
     the audience makes a program
     selection, choose Forever as the
     Loop #.

7   Preview the menu with its new
     background audio by right-clicking
     in the Menu viewer and choosing
     Preview from Here. We will talk
     more about the Project Preview
     window in "The Project: Building
     the DVD".

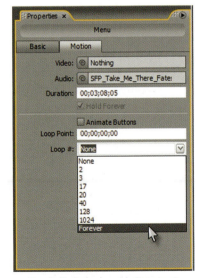

**Controls for menu background
audio in the Properties panel**

Adding Background Video to a Menu

Almost all commercial DVDs use background video and audio in their menus to really boost the entertainment value of the DVD. You can do the same for your DVD projects. The background video can be a short clip from the main program, a colorful, organic motion background, or just about any other video clip that you feel would fit the mood and style of the DVD. Adding background video to your project menus instantly takes your DVD from ordinary to extraordinary. A DVD menu with a video background is called a *motion menu*.

We've already seen how to add background audio to a menu. The way to add background video to a menu is very similar:

1   In the Project panel, select the menu to which you want to add background video.

2   Select the tab for the Properties panel to bring it forward in its frame.

3   Select the Motion tab in the Properties panel.

4   In the Video control, drag the pickwhip to a video asset that is visible in the Project panel. The pickwhip is the little swirl icon in the Video control. The target video asset will be outlined in gray as the pickwhip passes over it.

5   The name of the target asset will be added to the Video control. The length of the asset will be shown in the Duration control. If you only want part of the asset to play, you can manually enter the duration. The timecode displayed in the Duration control is in the same HH;MM;SS;FF format as the timecode in the Timeline viewer and the Monitor panel.

6   If you want to hear the audio from the video asset while the video plays in the menu, you also have to drag the pickwhip from the Audio control to the video asset.

7   To add a video asset and its audio as a menu background at the same time, hold down the (Alt) key and drag the video asset from the Project panel to the Menu viewer instead of using the pickwhip from the Properties panel.

8 From the drop-down list in the Loop # control, select how many times you want the video to loop before it stops. If you want the video to continue looping until the audience makes a program selection, choose Forever as the Loop #.

To preview a motion menu, you have to render it first. Recall that all menu objects, buttons, background images and background video must be flattened into a single video layer in order for the DVD to be built. By adding a video background to a menu, you are essentially compositing the video background underneath the menu objects. Each frame of the background video must have the menu buttons and any other menu objects superimposed on top of it. This composited menu has to be rendered before it can be previewed. To render a motion menu:

1 Right-click in the Menu viewer and choose Preview from Here. During the preview, which will display a static frame until the menu is rendered, click on the Render Current Menu button at the bottom-left of the

**The Project Preview window showing the
Render Current Menu button**

Project Preview window. "The Project: Building the DVD" has more information about the Project Preview window.

2   The Render Progress dialog will keep you updated on the status of the render. Be aware that Encore will transcode an untranscoded asset that is used as a menu background before rendering the menu. The transcoding of the asset may take a while.

If you want to render all of your motion menus at the same time, choose File ▶ Render ▶ Motion Menus.

Note: If you add background audio and background video that are different lengths to a menu, then the menu duration will be automatically set to the length of the asset most recently added. If audio is longer than video, then the last frame of the video asset will be displayed until the audio finishes. If video is longer than audio, then the audio portion will be silent until the video finishes. It's probably best if you use audio and video assets that have the same duration.

Saving Your Work for Use in Future Projects

Once you have created one or more menus in a project, you can use the Library to save those menus for use in other Encore projects. Adobe Encore DVD 2.0 has increased the flexibility available to the DVD author for adding entire menus to the Library. You can now add a menu to the Library as a Standard Menu or as a Menu Template. The new Menu Template option is especially useful for adding motion menus to the Library. A Menu Template file contains pointers to the audio and video assets that are part of the motion menu. The next time you create a menu from that Menu Template, Encore automatically adds the audio and video assets that are part of the motion menu to the project, and sets up the appropriate links (including duration and loop point) in the new menu.

To add a menu to the Library:

1   In the Library panel, choose the Set where you want the menu to be saved from the Set drop-down list.

2   Drag the completed menu from the Project panel to the Library panel.

3   Choose Standard Menu or Menu Template in the dialog box that appears.

4 If you choose Standard Menu, the saved menu will appear in the list of available menus as a Photoshop .psd file when you click OK.

5 If you choose Menu Template, you have the option of checking the Self-Contained box. Saving a menu as a Self-Contained Menu Template adds a copy of the video and audio assets to the template, which allows you to delete the original assets when the current project is complete. If you don't plan to delete the original assets, then leave this box unchecked to save disk space. The saved Menu Template will appear in the list of available menus as an .em file when you click OK.

The Add Menu dialog that appears when you drag a project menu to the Library panel

Note: If you save a motion menu as a Standard Menu, a single frame of the background video will be saved as the menu's background. The rest of the video, and any audio, will be lost.

At this point in the project, we have assembled all of the content that will be part of the main program and created all of the menus that we will need to allow the audience to navigate around the finished DVD. We've worked hard designing the menus and creating the timelines, but the menus aren't yet functional and the timelines are not readily available to the audience. Now it's time to hook everything up so that our finished DVD will function according to the plan contained in our flowchart.

One way to think about what we have done so far and what we have to do next is to take a good look at our flowchart once again.

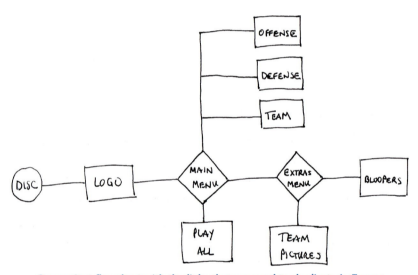

Our project flowchart with the links that we need to duplicate in Encore

We have created all of the boxed elements of our flowchart. Now we need to create the links between the elements that are represented by the connecting lines in the flowchart. We will also create links that aren't on the flowchart. The function of these omitted links is to create a complete circuit between all of the program content and menus so that the audience doesn't end up at a dead-end. Said another way, the links shown in the flowchart show us how to get to the program content and other menus, but we will need to add the links the get us back to where we started.

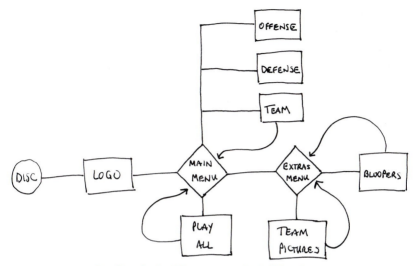

Our flowchart with some round-trip links shown

The Navigation Design Workspace

Adobe Encore DVD 2.0 has a new flowchart feature that can help us link up our project and make it look like the hand-drawn flowchart that we have used since starting to plan the project. The Flowchart panel is front-and-center in the Navigation Design workspace. We'll switch to that workspace now.

Before we get too involved in setting links using the Flowchart panel, we need to make sure that the icon thumbnail images that represent project elements are giving us useful information. Notice in the screenshot for the Navigation Design Workspace that the thumbnails for some of the project element icons are black. Having several icons that look the same in the Flowchart panel can slow down your work quite a bit, and may even induce errors. You can fix this problem by setting visually distinct poster frames for each chapter marker in each timeline in the project. Setting poster frames for chapter markers is discussed in "The Project: Timeline Creation".

We will use the Flowchart panel a lot as we link project elements together. Each type of link that we create will be represented in the panel. The Flowchart panel contains a wealth of information about project elements and their links. As we go along, we will discuss the kind of information that is available.

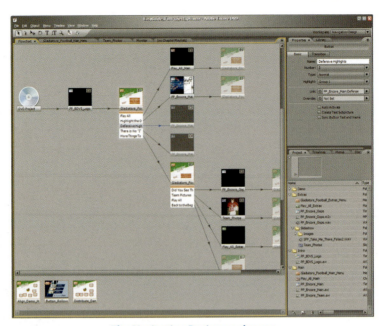

The Navigation Design workspace

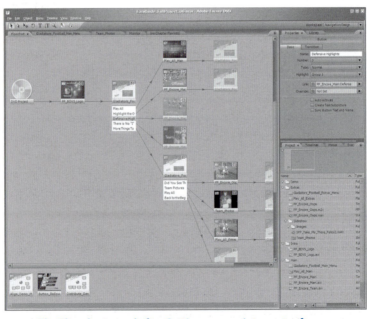

The Flowchart panel after Setting appropriate poster frames
in the different timelines

As with many operations in Encore, there are alternate ways to set up links. We got a taste of them when we added video and audio as menu backgrounds in "The Project: Menu Design and Creation". From the Properties panel for a project element, you can set a link by using the pickwhip for the appropriate control, or by selecting an item from the control's drop-down list. We will use these methods for those cases where we can't do everything we need from the Flowchart panel.

Setting a link using the pickwhip from the Properties panel

First Play

A DVD player needs to know what to do when a disc is first inserted into the player. The player looks for the project element marked as *First Play*. All DVDs require a project element to be set as First Play. Because of this requirement, Adobe Encore DVD 2.0 will automatically set First Play to be the first project element that you create in a new project. Generally, that won't be what you want as First Play, so you will need to reset the First Play link. Here's how:

1 Choose the Selection tool (V) from the toolbar.

2 Select the Disc icon in the Flowchart panel by clicking on it. Notice as you move the cursor into the top portion of the panel that the cursor changes to an arrow with a pickwhip icon. Clicking and dragging from one project element to another using this cursor will set a link between the two objects. The project element that you link "from" is called the *origin* of the link. The element that you link "to" is called the link's *target*.

3   Currently, the PP_Encore_Oops timeline is set as First Play in our project because it was created first when we imported that video asset as a timeline. Notice that the Link Line from the Disc icon to the First Play element is blue. A blue Link Line indicates that the origin of the link is selected; in this case it's the Disc icon. The blue Link Line is sometimes the best indication of which element is currently selected in the Flowchart panel.

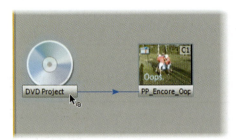

The DVD Project root disc icon is currently selected, as indicated by the blue Link Line between it and its target timeline. Notice the appearance of the Selection tool cursor in the Flowchart panel

4   Drag the cursor from the Disc icon to the element in the Flowchart panel's orphan area that you want to set as First Play. For our project, we want First Play to be the PP_BDVS_Logo timeline.

5   Notice that the Flowchart panel now has the Disc icon linked to the desired First Play project element, and that element is no longer listed in the orphan area. The project element that used to be set as First Play is not linked to anything, and has been returned to the orphan area of the Flowchart panel.

6   First Play in the Project panel is indicated by a small arrow inside of a yellow circle that is attached to the icon for the project element that has been designated as First Play.

End Actions

An *End Action* in Encore is a specific kind of link command that tells the DVD player what to do when whatever is playing now is finished. Any project element

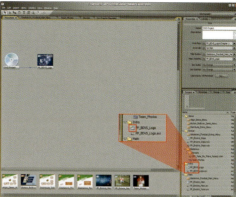

The First Play project element is linked to the Disc icon in the Flowchart panel, and indicated by a special icon in the Project panel

that contains or plays program content has an End Action that needs to be set. Although menus have their End Actions set to Stop by default, timelines and other project elements do not. To avoid potential navigation problems for the audience, you should explicitly check and set the End Action link for each element in the project.

Here are the End Actions available in Encore:

The End Action for the timeline is Not Set. This can cause navigation problems if not corrected prior to building the project

1 *Another project element*: This tells the DVD player to go to something else in the project – another timeline or a menu, for example.

2 *Link Back to Here*: This tells the DVD player to repeat whatever just finished playing. This choice is very useful for playing program content from a DVD player that will be left unattended for playback, such as information kiosks and advertising displays.

3 *Return to Last Menu*: This tells the DVD player to go back to the menu from which playback was initiated.

4 *Stop*: This tells the DVD player to enter the stop mode, just as if the audience had pressed the Stop button on the DVD player's remote control.

5 *Specify Link*: This brings up the Specify Link dialog, where you have complete control over the origin link and its target, including all audio and subtitle tracks.

To set the End Action for a project element:

1 Choose the Selection tool (V) from the toolbar.

2 Select the element in the Flowchart panel that you want to be the origin of the link.

3 Choose a target element. For a target element that is in the orphan area of the Flowchart panel, drag the cursor to the target. Notice that the target element has been removed from the orphan area and that the new Link Line is blue. Link Lines between other elements should be black.

4 For a target element in the top portion of the Flowchart panel, drag the cursor to the target. If the target is a menu, its buttons will be exposed in a list beneath the icon for the menu, and you can drag the link to a specific button, if desired. Again, the new Link Line should be blue, with other Link Lines black.

5 For the options Link Back to Here, Return to Last Menu and Stop, you must use the drop-down list in the Properties panel.

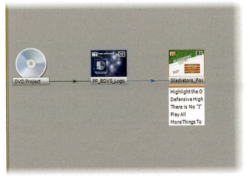

After setting a link in the Flowchart panel, the Properties panel will update the End Action control for the project element that is the origin of the link.

A menu in the Flowchart panel has its button list exposed

Note: Setting the End Action of a menu is useful for kiosks and other interactive displays. By combining menu duration with an End Action, you can specify a period of inactivity on a given menu that will trigger the End Action and return the display to the main menu, ready for the next visitor. Make sure to uncheck the Hold Forever checkbox in the Properties panel for the menu, or the DVD player in the display will ignore the menu duration and prevent the End Action from executing.

Auto Layout

As you set more and more links, the element icons and the Link Lines will take up more space in the Flowchart panel. Encore automatically rearranges the icons and the Link Lines to keep the

Using the drop-down list to set the End Action for a timeline to Link Back to Here. This will force the DVD player to repeat the current timeline

The updated End Action control in the Properties panel after setting a link in the Flowchart panel

Flowchart panel's working area as uncluttered as possible. If you decide that you need the icons arranged differently than Encore's automatic layout, select the Move tool (M) from the toolbar and rearrange the icons as desired. If you get to a point where you've made a mess out of the layout, all you have to do is right-click in an empty area of the panel and choose Auto-Layout All. Encore will arrange everything for you again, all nice and neat. Be sure to go back and choose the Selection tool (V) if you want to set more links in the Flowchart panel.

Menu Buttons

A menu button Link, like a timeline End Action, is a command that tells the DVD player where to go next. The difference is that an End Action only executes when the origin project element finishes playing, while a button Link executes as soon as it is activated. The most common way for a menu button Link to be activated is for the audience to press the Enter key while the button is selected. You set button Links in the Flowchart panel the same way that you set End Actions – by dragging with the Selection tool from the origin button to the target project element.

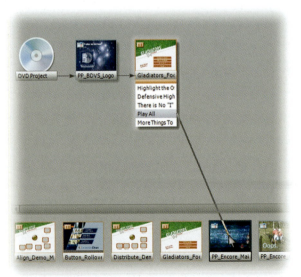

Dragging from the origin menu button to the target project element

When you create links for menu buttons using the Flowchart panel, it is important to make sure that only the button that you want to link, and not the whole menu, is selected. Otherwise, you will set the End Action for the menu and not the Link for the button. The project element icons that represent menus have two ways to indicate what is selected:

1 If the whole menu is selected, the list of buttons will be highlighted in light blue. Link Lines extending from any of the buttons that are already linked will be blue. You select the whole menu by clicking on its thumbnail.

2 If just one button on a menu is selected, the name of that button will have a gray highlight in the list of buttons. If the button is already linked, only that Link Line will be blue. You select an individual button by clicking on its name in the button list.

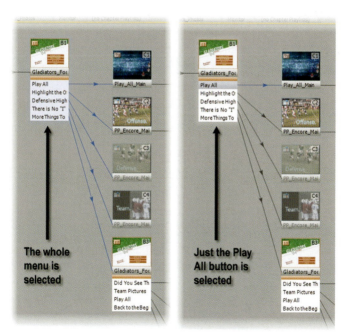

Different selections in a menu icon

There are some special target links for menu buttons that can't be set up by using the Flowchart panel. To set up those links, we need to use the drop-down list for the Link control in the Properties panel, similar to the way they are set for End Actions. Here's what those links do when they are applied to menu buttons:

1   *Resume*: This link is used to get the audience back into the program after playback of program content has been interrupted. If a button with a Resume link is activated, the DVD player returns to the point where playback was interrupted and begins playback again. This is a good button Link to have on a Subtitle or Audio Setup menu so that after the audience chooses an audio or subtitle track, they can get right back to watching the program from where they left off.

2   *Stop*: It's the same as for a Stop End Action. The DVD player enters the stop mode, just as if the audience pressed the Stop button on the DVD player's remote control.

3   *Link Back to Here*: When activated, the button Link points right back to the button itself. You might use this for buttons on duplicate or dummy menus when setting up a special effect like an Easter Egg, and you want to prevent the audience from leaving the menu until they find and activate the correct button. We'll talk more about duplicate menus and Easter Eggs in the Advanced Design Techniques section of this chapter.

4   *Specify Link*: The only way in Encore to give the audience access to subtitles or to additional audio tracks is through the Specify Link dialog. You would set this Link option for a menu button to allow the audience to select foreign language subtitles or a director's commentary, for example.

Sync Button Text and Name

Every new Encore project opens with a feature called Sync Button Text and Name enabled by default. Sync Button Text and Name is new to this version of Encore. It comes in handy when you are designing menus, because modifying the text that is part of a button's layer set automatically updates the name of the button to match the new text that you entered. You won't end up with the "Defensive Highlights" button showing up in the Menus, Properties and Flowchart panels as "Button 3". But this same feature is deadly when setting the button's link because the name of the button is also automatically updated to

**Linking a menu button to subtitle track 1 of a timeline by
using the Specify Link dialog**

the name of the target project element. I recommend disabling this feature for
each and every button on every menu in your project once you finish the menu
design and before you start setting up links. Otherwise, you can end up with
more than a few unpleasant surprises when you Preview your project later. To
disable Sync Button Text and Name for all buttons on all menus:

1 Click on the Menus tab to bring the Menus panel forward in its frame.
You will have to go to Window ▶ Menus if the Menus panel isn't open.

2 Make sure the Properties panel is open and forward in a different frame
than the Menus panel.

3 Select a menu from the top pane of the Menus panel.

4 Select all of the buttons in the button list in the lower pane of the Menus
panel.

5 Uncheck Sync Button Text and Name in the Properties panel to disable
this feature for all of the buttons on the selected menu at once.

6 Repeat steps 3–5 for each project menu.

169

Video Thumbnail Buttons

In many commercial DVDs, the buttons on a scene selection menu will include small thumbnail video clips of the chapter or scene to which the button links. In Adobe Encore DVD 2.0, *video thumbnail buttons* provide this same capability for your projects. Video thumbnail buttons can also be used to display static images of their links. Let's briefly revisit the Menu Design workspace and take a look at the menu that we used to demonstrate the Align and Distribute commands

The Sync Button Text and Name checkbox

in "The Project: Menu Design and Creation". We will use this menu to see how to set up links for a video thumbnail button.

A project menu with video thumbnail buttons. The layer set for the "Season 4" button is expanded in the Layers panel

There are some special properties of video thumbnail buttons that you need to keep in mind:

1 A video thumbnail button has to have a layer in the button layer set that is designated as the video placeholder layer. Encore knows that a layer is a video placeholder when it has the (%) prefix in the layer name. Button layer sets and prefixes are discussed in "The Project: Menu Design and Creation".

2 The size of the video that is displayed in the button thumbnail is determined by the size of the video placeholder layer in the button layer set. You can change the size of this layer and of the other button layers using Encore's normal resizing tools.

3 A video thumbnail button can only display the video from the timeline to which it is linked. You can't link the button to one timeline and display the video from another.

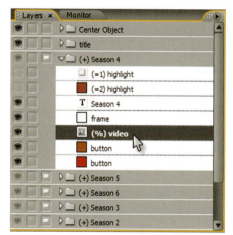

The video placeholder layer in the button layer set

To set the link for a video thumbnail button:

1 Click on the Timelines tab to bring the Timelines panel forward in its frame. If the Timelines panel is closed, use Window ▶ Timelines to open the panel. Scroll in the panel until the target timeline for the link is visible.

2 Click on the target timeline to open its chapter list in the lower pane of the panel.

3 Select the button to be linked in the Menu viewer.

4 In the Properties panel, drag the pickwhip for the Link control to the target chapter in the Timelines panel.

5   If there is a poster frame set for the target chapter, then Encore will
    display the poster frame in the button thumbnail. Otherwise, Encore
    will show the chapter's actual first frame.

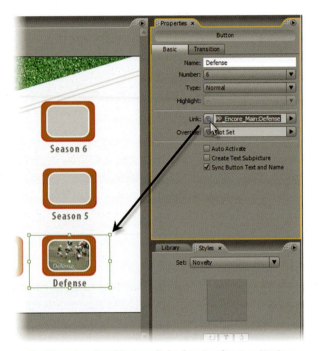

**A video thumbnail button linked to its chapter. Notice
how, with Sync Button Text and Name selected, setting
the link also changes the name of the button**

If you want the video thumbnail button to display a moving video instead of just
a still frame, you need to check the Animate Buttons checkbox in the Properties
panel for the menu. Here's how:

1   Bring the Project panel forward in its frame by clicking on the Project tab.

2   Click on the active menu in the Project panel. This loads the menu
    properties into the Properties panel.

3   Click on the Motion tab for the menu in the Properties panel.

4   Place a check mark next to Animate Buttons.

Note: The Animate Buttons checkbox is a global setting for all video thumbnail buttons on a particular menu. They all have to be animated, each showing thumbnail video clips, or they all have to display static images. You can't mix-and-match.

If you want playback in a video thumbnail button to start at a point other than the first frame of the linked chapter, then you must set a poster frame for that chapter at the point that you want playback to begin.

If the menu also has a motion background, then menu duration affects how the video thumbnails are played back. If menu duration exceeds the length of the video that is linked to the button, then the video thumbnail button will loop back to the beginning of the chapter (or back to the

Place a check mark next to Animate Buttons to have video thumbnail buttons play a video clip instead of just displaying a static frame

poster frame) as many times as necessary until the menu duration expires. For menus with a static background that is set to Hold Forever, the video thumbnails will loop indefinitely until the audience makes a selection.

Remote Buttons

The *Title* and *Menu* buttons on a DVD player's remote control are used to interrupt program playback and take the audience to a menu where one or more additional selections can be made. A second press of the Title or Menu buttons returns the audience to the point where playback was interrupted. The Title button may also appear on the player's remote control as the *Root Menu* button or the *Top Menu* button.

The Title Button link, which is set from the Properties panel for the Disc, controls where the DVD player is supposed to go when the Title button on the player's remote is pressed. To set the link for the Title Button:

1   Select the Disc icon in the Flowchart panel.

2   Bring the Properties panel forward in its frame.

3 Drag the pickwhip in the Title Button control to the target project element in the either the Flowchart panel. Typically, this link is set to the project's main menu.

The Menu Remote link is set from the Properties panel for a timeline or for a chapter playlist. This link controls where the DVD player goes when the Menu button on the player's remote control is pressed. In most cases, you will not need to change this link from its default target of Return to Last Menu. If you do decide to specify a different target for this link, here's how to set the Menu Remote link for a timeline:

The Title Button control

1 Select a timeline or a chapter playlist in the Flowchart panel.

2 Bring the Properties panel forward in its frame.

3 Drag the pickwhip from the Menu Remote control to the target project element in the Flowchart panel.

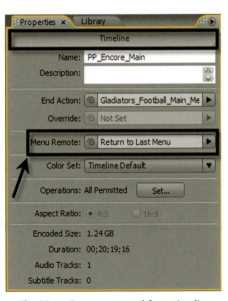

Playlists

The new Chapter Playlist feature in Adobe Encore DVD 2.0, combined

The Menu Remote control for a timeline

with the standard Playlist feature introduced in earlier versions of Encore, puts virtually unlimited control at your fingertips to quickly, easily and intuitively construct multiple program viewing paths. Playlists provide the standard playback functions that viewers have come to expect from high-quality commercial DVDs. We'll add those functions to our example project. Because of the incredible flexibility that Playlists give the DVD author, you can construct program viewing paths that, when made available to the audience, will keep the DVD fresh and exciting even after multiple viewings. Program content and your imagination are the only limiting factors as you decide how to present the program to the audience. We'll talk about standard Playlists first, and then discuss the new Chapter Playlists.

A standard Playlist is used to link timelines in the project to play in any order that the author wants. Much like adding audio assets to a Slideshow, you create a new Playlist and then add timelines to it, one at a time, in the order that you want them to play. If needed, you can create multiple Playlists from the timelines in a project, with each Playlist setup to play back different timelines in different orders. To create a Playlist:

1 Bring the Project panel and the Properties panel forward in their frames.

2 Click on the New Item button at the bottom of the panel and select Playlist. Give the new Playlist a name when prompted.

3 In the Properties panel for the new Playlist, at the upper right corner of the large, empty Timelines control you will see a pickwhip and a button for a flyout menu. Use either one to select the first timeline that should be put in the new Playlist. If

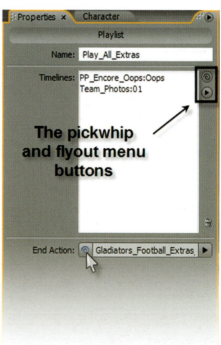

The Properties panel for a standard Playlist

the selected timeline has multiple chapters, you can choose the chapter that you want as the starting point for playback.

4 Repeat until you have added all of the desired timelines to the new Playlist.

5 Be sure to set the End Action for the new Playlist.

6 The new Playlist is now a separate project element like a timeline or a menu, and you can link to it from other project elements.

We'll use the Playlist feature to give the Extras Menu in our example project a Play All function by setting the Link for the Play All button on that menu to the new Playlist.

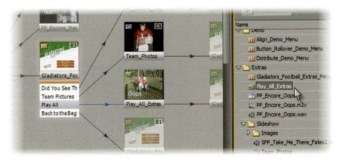

The new Playlist in the Flowchart panel and the Properties panel

A Chapter Playlist works a lot like a standard Playlist, the big difference being that it provides playback of individual chapters in a single timeline rather than playback of individual timelines in a project. You can set up a Chapter Playlist to play chapters in sequence like they appear in the timeline that is the source for the Chapter Playlist, or you can use a Chapter Playlist to play the chapters in any order that you want. A single timeline can have multiple Chapter Playlists, each one playing the chapters in a different order. To set up a Chapter Playlist from the chapter markers in a timeline:

1 Bring the Project panel forward in its frame.

2 Click on the New Item button at the bottom of the panel and select Chapter Playlist.

3 Choose a timeline from the dialog box that appears and click OK. A Chapter Playlist viewer will open in its frame. Like the Timeline, Menu and Slideshow viewers, the Chapter Playlist viewer can have multiple instances of itself open at one time.

4 From the left pane of the Chapter Playlist viewer, drag chapters to the right pane in the order that you want them to play. If the chapters are sorted in the left pane of the viewer in the desired order, then you can move them quickly to the right pane by selecting all of the desired chapters and then clicking on the Add button that is centered in the divider between the two panes.

5 When all of the desired chapters have been added, make sure to set the End Action for the Chapter Playlist. You can now link to the new Chapter Playlist from other project elements.

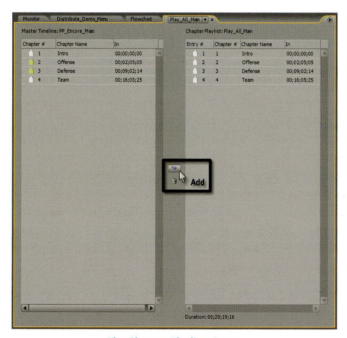

The Chapter Playlist viewer

Note: Due to the limitations of the DVD specification, there will be a short pause between timelines when they are played back using a standard Playlist. The length of this pause, and how noticeable it will be to the audience, is dependent on the brand of the DVD player that is used to play the finished DVD. There will also be a pause between chapters in a Chapter Playlist if the chapters are played out-of-sequence. Chapters played sequentially in a Chapter Playlist should not have any pauses between them.

Chapter Marker End Actions

Sometimes a DVD author will want the audience to be able to view chapters of a timeline individually – that is, the audience will select a chapter, watch it, and then be returned to a menu so that they can make another chapter selection. This is often the case with DVDs of concerts, plays, sporting events and other performance videos. But the author will also want the audience to be able to see the program in its entirety. We'll talk about how to set End Actions for individual chapter markers, and then we'll use those chapter marker End Actions and a Chapter Playlist to construct individual chapter playback and entire program playback for our project.

A chapter marker End Action tells the DVD player where to go next when a chapter in a timeline is finished playing. You set the End Action for the chapter marker, which is at the beginning of the chapter, but the End Action doesn't execute until the entire chapter finishes playing. If you were paying attention during our earlier discussion about End Actions in general, I can hear you saying to yourself now, "Okay, Okay. I get it. The chapter marker End Action executes at the end of the chapter." But the first time you try to set an End Action for a chapter marker in a timeline where you want chapters one and two to play, then return to a menu before chapter three plays, you're going to try to set the End Action for chapter three instead of chapter two. And when you Preview the project and the navigation doesn't work right, you will remember this paragraph and you will fix the problem. And then you'll thank me. You're welcome. Here's how to set the End Action for a chapter marker:

1   This is easiest from the Timeline Editing workspace, so we'll switch to that workspace now.

2   Bring the Project panel and the Properties panel forward in their frames.

3   In the Project panel, double-click the timeline that you want to edit. It will open in a Timeline viewer.

4   In the Timeline viewer, select a chapter marker for which you want to set an End Action. Notice that the marker turns red to indicate that it is selected.

5   In the Properties panel, use the pickwhip or the drop-down list for the End Action control to link to a Project element in the Project panel.

6   Repeat for each chapter marker that you want to have an End Action. Unselected chapter markers that have End Actions set are colored yellow in the Timeline viewer.

7   Return to the Navigation Design workspace if more project links need to be created.

The Timeline viewer showing chapter markers that are selected, unselected and those that have End Actions set

Note: You shouldn't set the End Action for the last chapter marker in a timeline because the End Action that is set for the timeline will link to the next project element. If the last chapter marker and its timeline both have their End Actions set, only the End Action for the last chapter marker will execute. Encore will warn you about this condition by flagging it as an error when you check your project.

We will add appropriate chapter End Actions to give our main program individual chapter playback, and we'll construct a Chapter Playlist for a Play All function.

Overrides

Let's start with a definition: a link *Override* in Encore changes the End Action of the target that is linked to by the End Action of the origin. I would say that again more slowly if I thought it would be less confusing, but it wouldn't be. What I will say is that in the past, link Overrides have caused more users more headaches in more Encore projects than just about any other feature of the program. That's because an Override doesn't affect the project element where the Override is set – it affects the element that is the target of the link that is being overridden. Using Overrides is like playing chess – you always have to think at least two moves ahead of what you are doing now.

But a new day has dawned! With the new features in Adobe Encore DVD 2.0, Overrides are no longer necessary to accomplish navigation tasks that used to require them in earlier versions of Encore. Those tasks now fall to Playlists and Chapter End Actions, both of which are very straightforward and intuitive. Overrides aren't completely obsolete, but you won't need them nearly as often, and the chances of introducing navigation and playback errors into your project will go way down if you avoid the use of Overrides. We'll examine a situation where Overrides are useful in the section on Advanced Design Techniques later in this chapter. In summary, I will say this: before you ever set any Override link, make sure you know exactly why you want to set it. Overrides are only needed in rare and special navigation situations where normal navigation links and Playlists cannot achieve the precise effect that you want. If in doubt at all, leave the Override control set to Not Set.

Setting Allowable User Operations

Have you ever popped a brand new, commercial DVD into your DVD player and been greeted by a slew of advertisements for other DVDs and future feature films? Did you ever wonder why, when you pressed the menu button on the player's remote control, the disc wouldn't take you to the main menu? Then, did you silently curse the studio for making you skip through (or even worse, sit through) all those ads? Well, the DVD specification allows a DVD author to disable a number of user operations at almost any point in the program. The studio that authored that new DVD disabled the Title and Menu remote buttons (and maybe the Previous/Next and Fast Forward/Rewind buttons, too!) during the presentation of the advertisements. And they almost certainly disabled all user operations during the display of the FBI anti-piracy warning. As a professional-level product, Adobe Encore DVD 2.0 supports enabling and/or disabling user operations. To set allowable user operations for a project element:

1 Bring the Properties panel forward in its frame.

2 Select the desired project element in either the Flowchart panel or the Project panel.

3 Click on the Operations: Set button in the Properties panel.

4 All user operations are permitted by default. To quickly disable all user operations, click the None radio button in the User Operations dialog.

5 Click the Custom radio button in the User Operations dialog enable the checkboxes next to the individual user operations for that project element. Different types of project elements have different sets of user operations.

6 Check or uncheck the available user operations as desired and click OK.

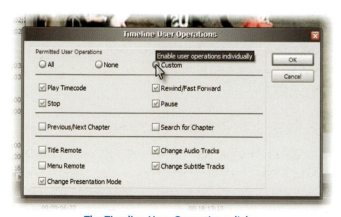

The Timeline User Operations dialog

Note: You cannot set allowable user operations for a standard Playlist. Each timeline in the Playlist will have its own set of allowable user operations.

Flowchart Panel Overview

Let's examine the Flowchart panel with all of our project links in place so that we can summarize the information that is available in this panel. We've already seen the icons and their thumbnails, representations of the project links and the button lists that accompany project menus. There is additional information in the icons that can help you readily identify link origins and targets, and assist you in identifying any navigational errors that may have crept in while you were creating the project links. Here is a summary of some of the additional information that is available in the Flowchart panel:

1   Aliases: You've probably noticed that some of the element icons in the Flowchart panel have a faded, semi-transparent look to them. Those icons are called *aliases*. An alias for a targeted project element indicates that element already appears somewhere else in the panel. Only the first occurrence of a project element in the Flowchart panel is displayed at full opacity. All other occurrences of that element will be displayed as aliases.

2   Type Icons: In the upper left corner of each element icon in the Flowchart panel is an icon that indicates the type of the project element – Timeline, Menu, Slideshow, Playlist or Chapter Playlist. These icons are the same ones that are used in the Project panel to indicate project element types.

3   Info Badges: In the upper right-hand corner of each element icon is an *info badge* that provides information about certain attributes of an element or the link to the element. Info badges indicate the default button on a menu and which button is the target of a link (B*n*), which chapter is the target of a link (C*n*), which audio and/or subtitle tracks are active (A*n* and S*n*), and if the subtitle track is off (SX).

Advanced Design Techniques

Most of the cool stuff that you see in commercial DVD menus (and in some of the special features on those DVDs) is done with creative use of multiple menus and subpicture highlights. It is important to note that commercial DVD authors are limited by the same DVD specification that you are. The biggest difference between spectacular Hollywood discs and DVDs that are a bit more ordinary is that experienced authors have found very creative ways to work with multiple

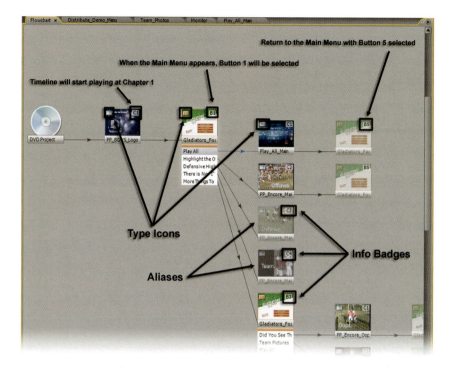

The Flowchart panel showing the visual clues that provide information about the project elements and their links

menus in a project. Sometimes, several menus are needed for just a single effect. We'll take a look at some of the most popular menu effects and provide methods to create those same effects inside of Encore.

Highlight-Only Menu Buttons

By far the most popular way for commercial DVD authors to create entertaining menu systems for their discs is to make everything except the subpicture highlights of the menu buttons part of the video background of the menu. Examples of commercial DVDs that employ this technique are *Lord of the Rings – The Fellowship of the Ring, Star Wars Episode One – The Phantom Menace, Shrek,* and *Harry Potter and the Sorcerer's Stone.* Recall that when Encore builds the project, everything in the menu except the subpicture highlights gets flattened into a single video layer. You can do the flattening yourself by creating the menu's background video in your own NLE, where you have complete control over the layout, compositing of button graphics, audio and any effects to be included in the video. All that remains inside of Encore is to add functional button highlights over the top of the background video. Here's how to do it:

1 Design your menu. Composite the menu graphics with video in your NLE and export it as a video clip with a frame size that Encore will import. Be sure to composite any graphics that you want to represent the menu buttons; the button graphics must be part of the video. Typical design elements for this type of menu include an introductory video clip that transitions into the full menu, static menu objects that are used to mask or overlay a looping inset video, and a transition video that is linked to by a menu button and then is subsequently linked to the program content.

2 In your graphics program, design a shape (or shapes) that will be used as a subpicture highlight for the composited menu buttons. If the Encore Library has shapes that fit the menu design, you can use the Library and eliminate an export/import step.

3 Import the background video into Encore as an asset. Add any highlight shapes to Encore's Library.

4 From the Library panel's General Set, add either the standard or widescreen Blank Menu to the project. Add the background video asset and any shapes to the menu. Each composited button graphic will need its own shape or copy of a shape for the subpicture highlights.

5 Convert the shapes to buttons and then hide or delete all of the button layers except for the subpicture layers. To hide a layer in a button layer set, click on the eyeball icon in the Show/Hide column of the Layers panel. If all you want are text buttons, then you can add the text and text subpicture highlights in Encore. All of the commercial DVDs listed above use text buttons in their menus.

6 In the Properties panel for the menu, select the Motion tab. Notice that the Video control links to the background video that you added. If the video asset contained audio, the Audio control also links to the background video. The Duration control should already be set to the length of the video.

7 Set the Loop Point control to the timecode that corresponds to when you first want the subpicture highlights to appear. Typically, this is just after the intro video transitions to the menu. When the menu is played back, the subpicture highlights will be disabled until the Loop Point is reached. Set the Loop # control to the number of times you want the menu to loop before the menu's end action is executed. Subsequent loops of the menu will start at the Loop point.

8 If the background video contains an intro that transitions to the menu, you will probably need a second copy of the menu that does not have the intro as part of the background video. That keeps the audience from having to watch the entire intro every time they navigate to the menu.

9 Audio cannot continue seamlessly between menus or when a menu loops, so good design dictates that, at the point you want the menu to loop, a quick fade out of the audio should be set up in your video or audio editing application. Consider doing something similar for the video content at the loop point.

10 Set button Links for the highlight-only menu buttons as desired.

Easter Eggs

Buttons on a menu are usually designed to provide clear and unambiguous directions to the audience on how to get to the program content that they want to watch. Sometimes however, DVD authors will purposely hide buttons that link to program content that can't be accessed any other way. As a reward, of sorts, for taking the time to thoroughly explore a disc's menus, the audience gets to see the extra goodies. Because the audience has to hunt for these hidden buttons, they are called *Easter Eggs*.

Highlight-only buttons are the preferred method for creating Easter Eggs. Here's how to quickly add and set up an Easter Egg in Encore:

1 As with other highlight-only buttons, decide on a graphic shape or text that will form the button highlight. Import your own or use a shape from Encore's Library.

2   Add the shape to a menu, choosing a location on the menu that is a little askew from where the audience may expect to find a button. Convert the shape to a button.

3   Turn on button routing in the Menu viewer and set up routing to the new button as desired. A popular choice is to have one, and only one, routing path that leads to the Easter Egg.

4   In the Layers panel, hide or delete all of the layers in the button layer set except for the subpicture layer.

5   Select or edit a Menu Color Set to give the Easter Egg button highlight the appearance that you want.

6   Set the Link for the new Easter Egg to the special program content.

If you want to get really sneaky, you can delete the subpicture layer from the Easter Egg button layer set so that the audience won't even know when they've navigated to the button! Their only clue that they have selected a hidden button will be that none of the other buttons on the menu are selected. Just make sure to hide, not delete, the other layers of the button layer set or the button won't work at all.

Button Rollover Menus

Imagine setting up a gardening web site that has a home page with a button on it, and that button contains a graphic of a flower bud. When a site visitor moves the mouse cursor over the button, the flower bud springs into full bloom. One click on the full-flower button and the visitor is whisked away to a different page of the site. Web-design software makes it fairly straightforward and relatively easy to create this *button rollover* effect for a web page.

The DVD specification doesn't allow for a fully functional rollover in DVD menus, but with a little imagination and some patience you can achieve almost the same effect by linking several menus together. The key to this effect is a menu button property known as *Auto Activate*. Normally, a button will not be activated until the audience first navigates to the button and then presses Enter on the DVD player's remote control. By setting the button to Auto Activate, the button will be activated as soon as the audience navigates to it.

To illustrate, we'll use the Astroturf Menu template as our main menu and the ZigZag Novelty style as our rollover effect:

1 Use duplicates of the main menu to create different rollover states. You will need a duplicate menu for every button on the main menu. Rename each duplicate menu to include the button number on the main menu that will link to it.

2 When all of the duplicate menus are created and named, use the desired rollover effect on each menu to modify the button that has the same number as the name of the menu. Only one button on each menu will be modified. For example, Button No. 2 on duplicate Menu No. 2 is the button that would be modified.

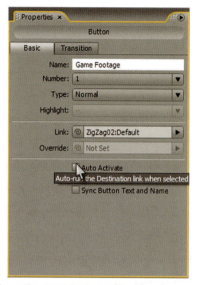

The Auto Activate checkbox for a button

The default button on the main menu has the desired rollover effect

3   On each menu, link the button that has the rollover effect to program con-
     tent. Link the remaining buttons on each menu to the duplicate menu that is
     numbered the same as the button. Just be prepared – that's a lot of linking.

4   Edit a new Menu Color Set
     to make the Selected and
     Activated states of all the
     button subpicture highlights
     transparent, except for the
     button that links to program
     content. For that button,
     make only the Selected state
     transparent. Use the
     independent controls for
     Highlight Group 1 and
     Highlight Group 2 to set up
     the different transparencies.
     Assign the appropriate
     Highlight Group to each of
     the menu buttons.

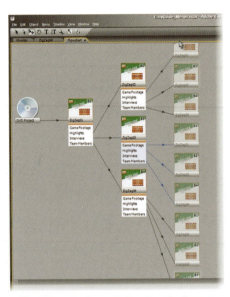

**The Flowchart panel showing the layout
for a simulated button rollover effect
using multiple menus**

Note: Since seamless audio and
video cannot continue across
different menus, you will need to give careful consideration to not using
background audio or background video on a button rollover menu. Still, if you
decide to use background audio and/or video, they need to be sufficiently
repetitive, and loop quickly enough, so as not to abruptly distract the audience
when they navigate to a button and playback is interrupted. The background
audio and video used on the main menu of the *Lemony Snicket's A Series of
Unfortunate Events* DVD is a good example of this. Click on the Mystery Button
during each of the different menu background videos, and then watch and listen
carefully as you are taken from menu to menu.

Trivia Quiz Games

You can use a series of menus to create a Trivia Quiz game for the bonus
material section of your project. Below is a flowchart that outlines a simple,

five-question quiz. The quiz is constructed entirely of menus. The rules of the quiz are as follows:

1   If the audience gets two wrong answers, they have to start the quiz over again.

2   If the audience misses only one question, then they can continue the quiz, but they can't get to the reward message.

3   If the audience gets all of the answers correct, they get to see a special reward message that isn't accessible any other way.

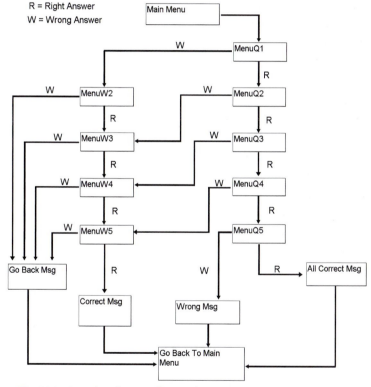

The Trivia Quiz Flowchart. Each menu has a question and three multiple-choice answers. The individual buttons for each of the three answers on a menu are not shown in the flowchart. MenuQ*n* are the questions in the correct-answer path and MenuW*n* are the questions in the second-chance path. Link lines labeled with an R indicate that a correct answer was given, while link lines labeled with a W indicate that a wrong answer was given

A menu-based Trivia Quiz is one case where link Overrides are useful. This quiz is also an outstanding example of why setting up disc navigation using Overrides can be very confusing. To see why, let's take a look inside Encore at the Flowchart panel for the finished quiz. Look twice because you probably won't believe that the Flowchart panel shown is really a representation of the completed quiz. Trust me, it is.

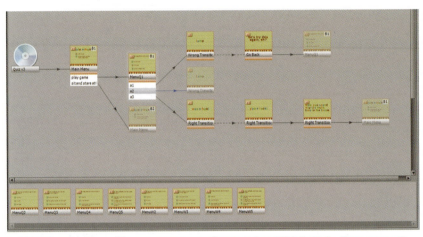

This Flowchart panel layout represents the completed Trivia Quiz. Every menu is accessible in some way during the quiz, but because link Overrides were used, many of the menus still reside in the orphan area of the Flowchart panel

Because the audience should have some immediate feedback as to whether a question was answered correctly or incorrectly, construction of the quiz in Encore will be a bit more complex than our planning flowchart shows. After each answer, a menu with a message indicating either a right or wrong answer should be shown. Use the Duration control to set how long the message should stay on-screen. These message menus would appear on the planning flowchart along each link line that is labeled R or W and that connects to another question menu. We could make multiple copies of each message menu, but if we use link Overrides then we only need one copy of each menu. Here is the menu design and link layout for the quiz:

1 Except for the first question, each question menu must be duplicated – we need one copy for the correct-answer path and one for the second-chance path.

2 Each question menu has a question and three possible multiple-choice answers. The two wrong answers are buttons that each link to a menu with a message indicating to the audience they answered incorrectly. When the audience answers incorrectly the first time, the wrong-answer indicator menu is displayed, and the audience is shifted to the second-chance path. This shift is invisible to the audience. A wrong answer from the second-chance path will show the wrong-answer indicator, followed by a message about having to start the quiz over again. At that point, the audience will be returned to the beginning of the quiz. The single correct answer on the menu is also a button, and it links to a correct-answer indicator menu. When the audience answers a question correctly, they continue on to the next question in the correct-answer path.

3 Since the wrong-answer indicator is a single menu that must be accessible from any question menu, the tricky part of the design is how to set the End Action for it. What happens when the menu duration for the wrong-answer indicator expires? If the audience gets to continue the quiz, then the target of the End Action would need to be different depending on which question was just answered. Since we won't know in advance which questions will be answered incorrectly, and since we can't change the End Action target on-the-fly during playback of the finished disc, the target can't be any of the question menus. But if the audience doesn't get to continue the quiz (because two questions have been answered incorrectly) then we have a fixed target that doesn't change: the start-over message menu. Therefore, the End Action target of the wrong-answer indicator needs to be the start-over message menu.

4 If the End Action of the wrong-answer indicator is the start-over message, how do we get the audience to the next question in the second-chance path when they've only missed one question? The solution is to use link Overrides. Recall that an Override doesn't affect the project element where the Override is set – it affects the element that is the target of the link that is being overridden. If that's still confusing, then let's put Overrides in the context of this quiz. If the audience is answering questions in the correct-answer path, an incorrect answer should display the wrong-answer indicator and then take them to the next question in the second-chance path. But the End Action link of the wrong-answer indicator is set to the start-over message, and we don't want the audience to go there just yet. We fix this by setting the Override control for the wrong-answer button that the audience selected on the question menu. The Link for that button is set to the wrong-answer indicator. By setting the target of the Override control for that same button to the next question menu in the second-chance path, we are telling Encore to link to the wrong-answer indicator, but then ignore the End Action of the indicator and go to the next question menu instead.

5   An analogous situation exists for the correct-answer indicator. The End Action target of the correct-answer indicator is the reward message. Skillful use of button Links and Overrides on the question menus will ensure that the audience never sees the reward message unless they answer every question correctly.

These are just a few examples of how to creatively use menus inside of Adobe Encore DVD 2.0 to construct special features and bonus material that will entertain and amaze your audience. Hopefully they will inspire you to explore the limits of your imagination as you author your own discs.

THE PROJECT:

Building the DVD

We need to get our project out of the computer and, ultimately, onto disc. That's the focus of this chapter. We'll examine the tools available in Adobe Encore DVD 2.0 that give you options for how best to do that. Whether you need just a few discs for a local client or hundreds of discs for nationwide distribution, Encore can produce the right finished product for the job.

Verify Project Settings

In "The Project: Transcoding", we told Encore what size of disc we would be using for our project. That took care of the only project setting that we needed until now. The other project settings are for the Region Code of the disc and for Copy Protection options. Let's take a look at the Project Settings dialog:

1   Select the tab for the Disc panel to bring it forward in its frame.

2   Click the Project Settings button.

3   Verify that the Disc Size is correct for the project.

The Project Settings dialog

4 Set Region Code and Copy Protection options only if you will build a DVD Master of the project by writing to a Digital Linear Tape drive. These options will only function on discs that are pressed at a replication facility. For a burned disc or a disc image produced by Adobe Encore DVD 2.0, setting these options will have no effect on the finished DVD. All regions will always be enabled and no copy protection will be available.

Checking the Project

Every Encore project needs to be checked for errors. Just as you would spell-check a word processor document before printing it, you should check your project for mistakes before building it. While we've been working on this project, Encore has silently been taking note of mistakes that it detects. Like a good administrative assistant, Encore won't let you push your project out the door without bringing those mistakes to your attention. If we try to go straight to building the DVD and Encore detects errors in the project, we get a reminder that these errors should be corrected before proceeding. Let's take a sneak peek at the Build DVD panel to see how this works:

1 Select the tab for the Disc panel to bring it forward in its frame.

2 Click the Build DVD button. If you can't see the Build DVD button in the Disc panel, press the (~) key to temporarily maximize the frame. The Build DVD panel opens in a floating window. If you want, you can dock the panel to a frame, or just leave it undocked as is.

3 Look at the bottom of the panel. If Encore has found any errors, there will be a small warning icon and a message that project errors have been detected. The message even includes a suggestion on what to do next – namely, use the Check Project function to view and correct the problems.

4 Close the Build DVD panel and press the (~) key again to put the workspace back the way it was.

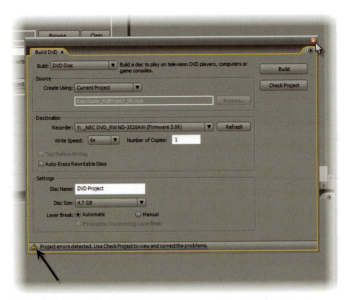

The Build DVD panel is undocked by default. Note the warning message at the bottom of the panel

Let's take Encore's advice and check the project to see exactly what's been found:

1   Click the Check Project button in the Disc panel.

2   The top section of the Check Project dialog lists all of the error types that Encore detects. They are loosely organized into three groups – navigational errors, menu and disc errors and timeline errors.

3   If the checkbox for an error type is selected, then Encore will specifically check for those kinds of problems. Encore defaults to having all error types selected. De-select any error types that you don't want Encore to identify. For example, if you showed excellent judgment by taking my advice and not setting any Overrides in your project, then you wouldn't need Encore to look for problems with Overrides when it checks the project. Still, the safest course of action is to check every project at least once with all error types selected.

4   Click on the Start button to begin error-checking the project.

The Check Project dialog. All error types are selected and ready for checking

Correcting Errors

When Encore is finished checking the project, the lower section of Check Project dialog will contain a list of the specific errors that were found, and which project elements have those errors. You can keep the Check Project dialog open and hovering above the other frames as a reference while you correct the listed errors. Although it can't be docked like other panels, the Check Project dialog behaves just like an undocked panel: select a project element in the dialog and its properties will appear in the Properties panel; double-click on a menu in the Check Project dialog and the Menu viewer will open with the selected menu loaded.

Sometimes the errors that Encore flags aren't really mistakes in the context of your project. In our project, for example, Encore lists three menus as being orphans and several buttons are flagged for their Links not being set. The menus and buttons listed in this case were included as part of the project only to illustrate certain features of Adobe Encore DVD 2.0 – they were never intended to link to program content. However, leaving them in the project is a bad idea. We'll delete these extra menus (and their buttons along with them) before we build the DVD.

Note: Make sure you delete any orphan timelines and menus that won't be part of the program. Encore will include the orphans on the finished disc if they're

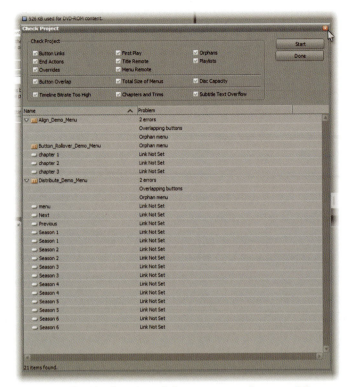

Keep the Check Project dialog open as a reference while you correct project errors

not deleted. Not only will this chew up valuable disc space, but it could be potentially embarrassing. Some DVD players have excellent Title search functions, and the audience may be able to stumble across an orphan timeline and view it by performing a Title search. A savvy audience can also find orphan menus by using a software DVD player on a computer.

Before we delete the orphan menus, let's take a look at an interesting error that appeared in the Check Project dialog. Two of our orphan menus are flagged as having overlapping buttons.

If those menus were going to be used in the project, that would be a fairly significant error. Overlapping buttons will prevent proper menu navigation on the

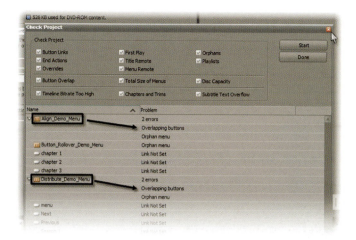

These menus have overlapping buttons

finished DVD, which will thoroughly confuse your audience. Let's see how to identify which buttons are overlapping and how to fix the problem:

1 Double-click a menu in the Check Project dialog that is flagged as having overlapping buttons.

2 Switch to the Menu Design workspace and move or resize the Check Project dialog to reveal the Menu viewer underneath.

3 Click on the Show Button Routing button at the bottom of the Menu viewer.

4 Notice that bounding boxes have appeared around each of the menu buttons. If any of these bounding boxes overlap, then the DVD player will get confused when the audience tries to navigate to one of the overlapping buttons. The audience will not be able to properly or consistently navigate around the menu.

5 To correct overlapping buttons, use the resizing and arranging techniques discussed in "The Project: Menu Design and Creation".

Generally, a good practice is to correct all errors before building the project. If you decide not to do that, be aware that Encore will continue to warn you about those errors any time the Build DVD panel is open.

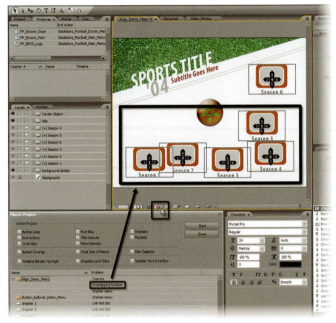

Overlapping button bounding boxes

Previewing the Project

Even if the Check Project dialog shows no errors after corrections have been made, that only confirms that the technical execution of the project design is sound. What if the finished project doesn't really do what you wanted when you were planning the disc? That's where Encore's project Preview function is helpful. You need to see if the completed project actually does what you intended when you started the project. The Preview function simulates a real-world DVD player, with the advantage that project assets don't have to be transcoded first, and you don't have to wait for several gigabytes of files to be written to disc. It's readily available at any time.

You don't have to check the project for errors before you preview it. In fact, you should preview parts of the project periodically at various stages of completion to evaluate design and execution. However, checking the completed project before previewing it gives you fewer things to worry about during the preview. Let's take a look at the project Preview window:

1 Select File ▶ Preview (Alt+Ctrl+Spacebar) or click the Preview button on the Toolbar to open the Preview window. Note that all other functions in Encore are disabled while this window is open.

2 The project starts playing immediately, with whatever is set to First Play. If no First Play element exists, Encore will warn you. If you still want to preview, you have to start the preview by clicking on the Play button. The project element that was created first will be played back in this case.

3 If the asset currently playing is untranscoded, the Transcode Status icon in the Preview window will be red. Transcoded assets will have a green Transcode Status icon.

4 The Preview window contains navigation controls that simulate those found on a DVD player. Use these controls to examine the playback of the project from start to finish. There are no Fast Forward or Rewind controls in the Preview window. If you want to skip rapidly through the preview, use the Next and Previous controls, or the Execute End Action button.

5 There are also controls to assist with the preview that wouldn't be found on a normal DVD player. If you see something you don't like about an asset that is currently playing, use the Exit Here button to leave the Preview function and load the current asset into its appropriate viewer for editing. The Exit and Return button will exit the Preview function and return you to where you were in the project before you started the preview.

Remember that the project Preview is a simulation of a real DVD player. As such, there are some differences between the Preview function and what you can expect to see when the finished disc is shown on a television:

1 When video playback loops, moves from one timeline to another, moves from a menu to a timeline or moves between menus, any pause in the playback will be much more pronounced in Encore's preview than in a normal DVD player. On better players, the pause may be so short that it will be undetectable.

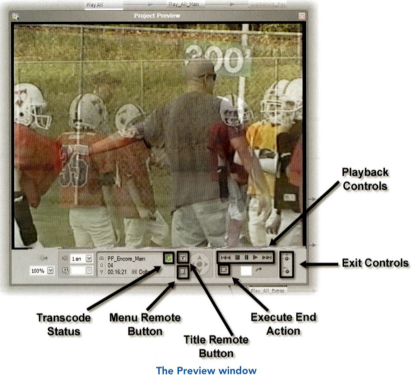

Playback Controls

Exit Controls

Transcode Status

Menu Remote Button

Title Remote Button

Execute End Action

The Preview window

2   It's possible for audio to be out-of-synch with the video during Preview. In most cases this condition will not be present on the finished DVD.

3   If a menu button links to the Resume function, it may not work right in Preview, but it will operate correctly on the finished disc.

4   Any interlacing artifacts that may appear in the Preview window only indicate that the video is interlaced – they don't allow you to discern if the interlaced fields are being displayed in the proper order. To determine if the production pipeline for the video introduced any field-order issues, you must test on an interlaced television.

Because of these and other limitations for the simulated playback of the DVD in Encore's Preview function, the only reliable, without-a-doubt verification that a project is designed and working correctly is to burn one DVD and test the actual disc in a normal DVD player. We'll discuss making a DVD disc shortly.

Note: While blank DVD-5 media is readily available and relatively inexpensive, it still doesn't make sense to waste discs. While you are testing, avoid the creation of *coasters,* or ruined blank discs, by purchasing a couple of blank DVD−RW and DVD+RW discs that can be used over and over again.

Once your project has been checked for errors, previewed and you are satisfied that everything is working as it should, it's time to build the DVD! There are several choices available in Encore for how to build the project, and each one serves a specific purpose. The goal of all of them, however, is to get your finished project out of the computer and onto disc.

Building a DVD Disc

Use the DVD Disc option when you're only going to burn a few copies of the disc. For wider distribution, use the DVD Image or DVD Master options. To build a DVD disc:

1   Click on the tab for the Disc panel to bring it forward in its frame.

2   Open the Build DVD panel by clicking the Build DVD button in the Disc panel.

3   Check that the DVD Disc option is selected in the Build control – it should be set to that by default.

4   Check that the Create Using control in the Source group is set to Current Project. That is the default setting. If you want to burn copies of a previously built DVD Image, then you would set this control to DVD Image and use the Browse button to navigate to the location of the image file.

5   Check the Destination group to make sure that the correct Recorder is selected, that the write speed is reasonable based on the type of media that you have and that the correct number of copies is specified. If you are building the project on an RW disc to test, you can select the Auto-Erase Rewritable Discs checkbox, and then if your RW disc is not blank, Encore will erase it for you without prompting. This feature allows you to order the disc to be built and then walk away from the machine while Encore goes to work. If you leave this box unchecked when using an RW disc that isn't blank, Encore will stop building the project and ask you if it's okay to erase the disc. You will have to answer the prompt before Encore will continue building the DVD.

6 Do a quick check of the Settings group to verify that the project's Disc settings are accurate.

7 Because we checked the project for errors earlier, there should be a reassuring message at the bottom of the panel that says our project is ready for building.

8 Click on the Build button and away we go. If any of the project assets still need transcoding, Encore will do that now.

9 When the disc is finished, Encore will eject the disc.

The Build DVD panel setup for building a DVD Disc

Dual-Layer Discs

If your DVD burner supports dual-layer media, then you can set up an 8.54 GB dual-layer project in Adobe Encore DVD 2.0. A dual-layer DVD has 2 layers of data on the disc, with the top layer being semi-transparent and offset vertically from the lower layer. When a DVD player reaches the end of the first layer, the laser re-focuses on the second layer and continues playback. There is sometimes a noticeable pause in playback while the laser re-focuses. Ideally, this *layer break* will occur in between timelines so that the pause normally associated with playback moving from one timeline to another can be used to re-focus the laser at the same time. This limits the number of interruptions to the audience's viewing experience. To set the layer break in Encore:

1   Open the Build DVD panel if it's not already open.

2   Verify that the Disc Size control in the Settings group is set to 8.54 GB dual layer.

3   Choose either the Automatic or Manual radio buttons for the Layer Break control and click the Build button to start building the project.

4   If you choose Automatic, Encore will attempt to place the layer break between timelines. If it can't do that, then it will place the layer break at the last chapter point within the legal range. The legal range dictates that the first layer must be of a longer duration than the second layer because of the way that the layers are written to disc. If there is no chapter point for Encore to use, then it finds the midpoint timecode of the project, sets a chapter marker there, and then sets the layer break to that new chapter marker. All of these occur behind the scenes, and Encore will build the project and not bother you with any of this layer break stuff. Very cool and very easy.

5   If you want some degree of control over where the layer break is placed, choose Manual. I say "some" degree of control because if Encore can put the layer break between timelines, it will do so without asking you first and then it will continue to build the project. If Encore can't put the layer break between timelines, then a dialog will pop open asking you where you want to set the layer break. This dialog identifies the timeline in the project where the layer break needs to be set. You are offered a choice between using a chapter point from that timeline and using a timeline timecode. Encore also provides the legal range for the timecode if you decide to use that option. Click OK and Encore will continue building the project.

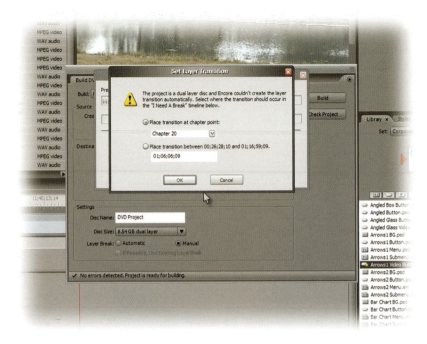

Options for setting the layer break in a dual-layer project

Note: If you are re-building a project in which you previously set a Manual layer break as a response to Encore asking you where you wanted it, then an additional layer break option becomes available in the Settings group: If Possible, Use Existing Layer Break. If you select this option, Encore will attempt to use the layer break point that was previously set. If the layer break point was previously set automatically by Encore, or if this is the first time you are building the project, then this option will not be available.

Building a DVD Folder

Building the project as a DVD folder allows for quick checking of the project on the computer by a software DVD player. The folder functions in the software DVD player just like a regular disc would. The DVD folder is not intended to be burned directly to disc because the finished DVD may not work right. Use the DVD Disc function to burn the project directly to disc. You can also use a DVD folder built with Encore in a third-party mastering application so that you can use that application's facility for setting the layer break in dual-layer projects. To build the current project as a folder on a hard drive:

1   Click on the tab for the Disc panel to bring it forward in its frame.

2   Open the Build DVD panel by clicking the Build DVD button in the Disc panel.

3   In the Build control, select DVD Folder.

4   The Source for the folder will always be the current project.

5   In the Destination group, click the Browse button and navigate to where you would like Encore to store the DVD folder after it is built.

6   Verify the correct project and layer break settings in the Settings group as needed. Look for the warm, fuzzy message at the bottom of the panel that tells us the project is error-free and ready for building.

7   Click on the Build button to start building the DVD folder. Untranscoded assets will be transcoded at this time.

The Build DVD panel setup to build a DVD Folder

Note: If you are an experienced DVD author, and you examine the folder structure for a DVD created by Encore, you may be surprised to find that the AUDIO_TS folder is missing. The AUDIO_TS folder is only for DVD-Audio discs, and is not required for DVD-Video. Encore doesn't create an AUDIO_TS folder for a DVD-Video project.

Building a DVD Image

If you intend to burn more than a few copies of the DVD, but are not planning on a run of several hundred, or if you will re-burn the DVD in multiple burning sessions, then building a DVD Image is the way to go. If you use the DVD Disc option, with the current project as the source for each re-burning session, then you have to wait for Encore to build any slideshows, rebuild the menu system and reorder the files before the burn can start. With a DVD Image as the source, all you have to do is load the image file and burn the discs. No waiting involved. DVD Image files are also useful if you plan to use a third-party mastering application to burn the discs. Often those applications will support burning to multiple DVD recorders simultaneously, a feature which Encore does not yet support. To build a project using the DVD Image option:

1   Click on the tab for the Disc panel to bring it forward in its frame.

2   Open the Build DVD panel by clicking the Build DVD button in the Disc panel.

3   In the Build control, select DVD Image.

4   For the Create Using control in the Source group, choose either Current Project (the default) or DVD Volume. Selecting DVD Volume lets you navigate to a location that contains a DVD Folder and then create a DVD Image of the folder. Unlike trying to burn a DVD Folder directly to disc, building an image of the folder in Encore will create a valid DVD Image file that can be safely burned to disc.

5   In the Destination group, click the Browse button and navigate to where you would like Encore to store the DVD Image file.

6   Verify the correct project and layer break settings in the Settings group as needed. Look for the message at the bottom of the panel that indicates the project is error-free.

7   Click on the Build button to start building the DVD Image. Untranscoded assets will be transcoded at this time.

The Build DVD panel setup to build a DVD Image

Building a DVD Master

Creating a DVD Master for a professional replicating facility is needed if you plan on distributing hundreds of finished DVDs. Recall that replication is also the only way to add copy protection to your discs. Any project that requires copy protection must be written as a DVD Master out to Digital Linear Tape, or *DLT*. Even if copy protection isn't required, DLT remains the preferred format for DVD Masters. To use the DVD Master option in the Build DVD panel:

1   Ensure that a DLT drive is connected to your computer via a SCSI interface.

2   Click on the tab for the Disc panel to bring it forward in its frame.

3 Open the Build DVD panel by clicking the Build DVD button in the Disc panel.

4 In the Build control, select DVD Master.

5 For the Create Using control in the Source group, choose Current Project.

6 In the Destination group, verify that your DLT drive is listed as an option in the drop-down list for the Recorder control. If it's not, click the Refresh button to force Encore to scan for your drive again.

7 Verify the correct project and layer break settings in the Settings group as needed. Look for the reassuring message at the bottom of the panel that indicates the project is error-free and ready for building.

8 Click on the Build button to start building the DVD Master. Untranscoded assets will be transcoded at this time.

Click the Refresh button if Encore doesn't list your DLT drive

Note: Encore doesn't include a utility for verifying that the project has been written correctly out to tape.

Adding DVD-ROM Content

You may want to put data on your finished DVD that can only be accessed by computer. For example, you might want supporting documents and supplemental photographs available as research material to students who will be watching your educational DVD. This extra data, available only from the desktop of a personal computer, is known as *DVD-ROM content*. To add DVD-ROM content to a project:

1   Organize all of your ROM content into a single folder on your hard drive.

2   Bring the Disc panel forward in its frame.

3   In the DVD-ROM Content group, click on the Browse button and navigate to the folder that contains the ROM content. Click OK.

4   Encore lists the folder for the content and updates the disc graphic with the space required for the added data.

DVD-ROM content has been added to the project

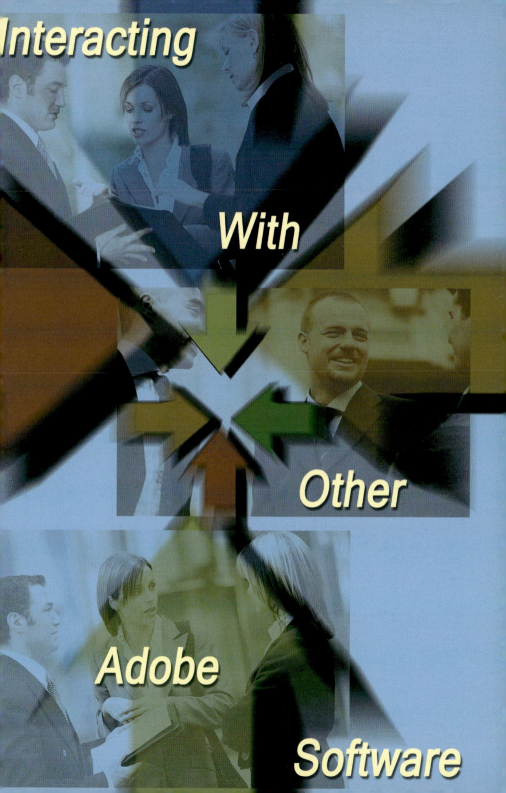

Interacting

With

Other

Adobe

Software

By using content created with other Adobe software packages in your DVD project, you can dramatically increase the entertainment value of your finished discs. With just a few mouse clicks inside of Encore, you can call up the Adobe software package that created the assets and elements used in your Encore project and begin editing or updating them. This tight integration is simply not available with any other DVD authoring program, and it represents tremendous flexibility and efficiency during the construction of your DVD project. The new Adobe Production Studio includes an exciting additional level of integration between Adobe Encore DVD 2.0 and Adobe After Effects 7.0 – the Dynamic Link. We'll discuss dynamic links when we talk about working with After Effects.

Note: The information in this chapter is not designed to be a primer on how to use other Adobe software. Proficiency in these other applications is assumed. This chapter focuses on how to use and edit the content that is created in other Adobe software packages while you are working inside of Encore.

The Edit Original Command

Sometimes a DVD author will find that an asset in the project must be re-edited to some degree. Artistic and timing concerns are often the cause. The Edit Original command in Encore uses the project link embedded in assets that were created in other Adobe software packages to call up the appropriate application and load the project that was the source of the asset, where changes can be made. After saving the changes and returning to Encore, the Encore project is updated immediately with the new version of the asset. The following screenshots show where to find the option to embed a project link in Adobe After Effects, Adobe Audition and Adobe Premiere Pro.

Note: You must overwrite the original file when saving changes during an Edit Original operation or Encore will never see the updated asset. Consider doing a Save As inside of the linked application before making any changes so that you can preserve the original version of the asset as a backup.

Working with Adobe Photoshop

At the heart of the integration between Encore and other Adobe software is the link between Encore and Adobe Photoshop. Inside of Photoshop, you can

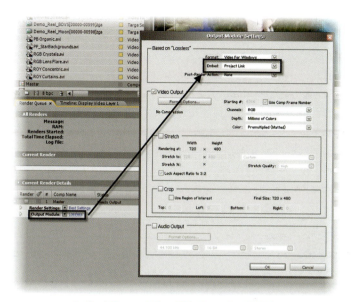

**Embedding an After Effects project link in
a rendered composition**

Embedding an Audition session link in an exported mixdown

create menus from scratch that have all of the bits and pieces that Encore needs to make the menu work on the finished DVD. By the time the menu from Photoshop gets into Encore, literally all that's left to do in Encore is link the menu to its assets and build the project. And opening an existing Encore

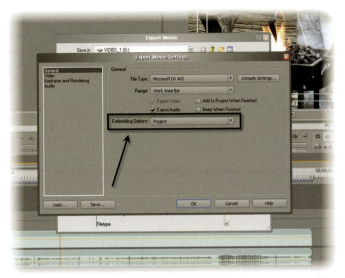

Embedding a Premiere Pro project link in an exported movie file

menu in Photoshop for editing is as simple as clicking a single button on the Toolbar.

Note: Encore integrates well with Adobe Photoshop version 6.0 or later. Versions of Photoshop before 6.0 have issues with Encore that are unpredictable, and for the most part, untested. I recommend upgrading to the latest version of Photoshop if your current version is earlier than 6.0.

The Edit Menu in Photoshop Command

If a menu from the Encore Library is generally a good fit for your project, but it needs a little tweaking, or if you need to make some changes to a menu that's already been added to the project, the Edit Menu in Photoshop command is a quick way to launch Photoshop and load your menu as the active document.

But wait a minute. We already know how to edit and customize a menu inside of Encore, so why make a big deal about the connection to Photoshop? It's important because the toolset in Encore is very limited compared to what is available inside of Photoshop. For example, you can't give layers or layer sets names with prefixes to add to or change the function of menu objects from inside of Encore, but you can do it from within Photoshop. Inside of Photoshop, you can pick apart each and every layer of the menu and edit it. This includes any vector masks or layer effects, neither of which is accessible in Encore. And getting back to work in Encore is a snap, because once you finish your edits, saving the menu document from inside of Photoshop automatically updates the menu inside of Encore. Here's how to send a menu to Photoshop for editing:

1   Select the menu in the Project panel.

2   Click on the Edit Menu in Photoshop button on the Toolbar (Ctrl+Shift+M). Encore launches Adobe Photoshop and loads the menu as the active document.

3   Make changes to the menu in Photoshop as required.

4   Inside of Photoshop, choose File ▶ Save (Ctrl+S). The menu is instantly updated in Encore.

Note: If you want to update the original file, Edit Menu in Photoshop essentially works opposite to the way that Edit Original works. A Photoshop file imported as a menu into Encore exists inside of Encore only as a copy of the original file. When you call up Photoshop to edit and update the menu from Encore, it is this copy that gets updated. To update the original file, you have to perform a Save As from inside of Photoshop and then overwrite the original file.

Creating Menus in Photoshop

Adobe Photoshop has a clear and distinct advantage over other graphics programs when it comes to creating menus for Encore. The layer sets, layers and special layer names from Photoshop translate directly to buttons and special-function button layers inside of Encore. Additionally, if you have a CS version of Adobe Photoshop, you can choose an image preset size that uses non-square pixels.

Here's how to get started creating an Encore menu inside of Photoshop:

1   Select File ▶ New.

2   Choose an image preset size that corresponds to the type of menu you are creating. There are labeled preset sizes for standard and widescreen in both NTSC and PAL. The CS versions of Photoshop have non-square pixel preset sizes available.

As you add layers and layer sets to the menu in Photoshop, use Encore's naming conventions to identify which layers will be video placeholders or subpicture layers, and which layer sets will be menu buttons. Here's a list of some of the more common layer-name prefixes:

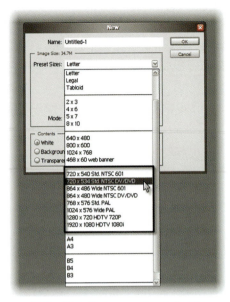

- (+) indicates to Encore that the layer set is a menu button.

- (=1), (=2) or (=3) indicates to Encore that the layer in a button layer set is a subpicture layer. Each of the numbers 1, 2 or 3 represent an available color in the subpicture highlight that will be generated in

Video-friendly image preset sizes in Adobe Photoshop 7

the DVD player when the finished disc is played back.

- (%) indicates to Encore that the layer in a button layer set is a video placeholder.

We'll see how to use more than one color for the subpicture highlight, and how to make video placeholder layers for video thumbnail buttons, next.

Additional Subpicture Highlight Colors

In "The Project: Menu Design and Creation" we talked about subpicture highlights, menu color sets and subpicture layers. We limited our discussion to the (=1) subpicture layer, which, in concert with a Menu Color Set, defines a single subpicture highlight color. But a DVD subpicture highlight can have up to three colors plus transparency. By naming layers in Adobe Photoshop using the proper prefixes, we get access to two additional colors for creating subpicture highlights. In Encore, these additional colors will be represented by the (=2) and (=3) layers in a button layer set. Let's take a look at how to do this using the

American Flag as a subpicture highlight. As you might expect, the three colors in our subpicture highlight will be red, white and blue:

1   In Photoshop, create a new image document using an appropriate video-friendly preset size.

2   Import or create an image of the American Flag to use as a selection or masking guide.

3   Use Quick Mask mode or the Selection tools to get each color into its own layer. The stars and white stripes of the flag will be on one layer, the background field for the stars will be on another layer and the red stripes will be on a third layer.

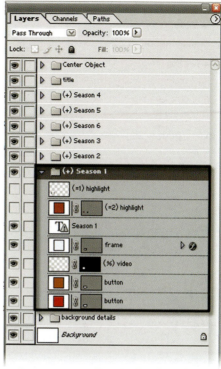

Layer-name prefixes in the Photoshop layers palette

4   Eliminate any color gradations by filling each of the three layers with the appropriate solid color.

5   Composite the three layers so that everything lines up properly and the composited image looks like a flag.

6   Create a new layer set and name it with a (+) prefix so that Encore will know it's a button when we import it. Move the three composited flag layers into the new

The filled individual layers for each of the three colors

layer set. Add additional button graphics and text to the new button layer set as desired.

7   Name the red layer with the (=1) prefix, the white layer with the (=2) prefix and the blue layer with the (=3) prefix. After we import the menu into Encore, those prefixes will indicate which subpicture layer should generate which subpicture highlight color.

8   Poke out the eyeball for each subpicture layer to turn off its visibility. All subpicture layers in Encore have to have their layer visibility turned off. Encore is smart enough to do this for you if you forget before importing the menu.

9   Add additional graphics and text to the rest of the menu as desired.

Note: In Photoshop, avoid using feathered masks or more complex layer effects on subpicture layers. The limited color palette available for the generated

The composited color layers with other graphics and text layers. The layers and layer sets have been properly named in preparation for import into Encore. The layer visibility for the subpicture layers is still on so that you can see how the subpicture highlight will look on the finished DVD

subpicture highlight can't handle the effects, and the highlights on the finished disc will not appear as you intended.

Note: If two subpicture layers overlap in Encore, opaque areas in the top layer act like a cookie-cutter for the bottom layer – any part of the overlapped layer that underlies an opaque area in the top layer is discarded. Because of this, you cannot use transparency in the Menu Color Set to simulate color changes or blending modes.

Video Placeholder Layers

In "The Project: Linking Everything Together" we saw how to make a video thumbnail button for a menu so that static or moving images of the chapter or

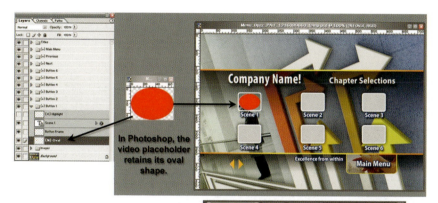

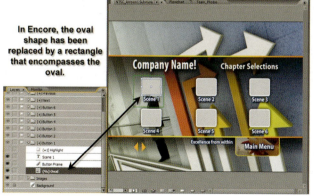

Without a layer or vector mask in Photoshop, the shaped layer loses its shape back in Encore

timeline that is linked to the button will be shown to the audience. Now let's take a look at how to create a video thumbnail button for a menu inside of Photoshop. A key part of a video thumbnail button is the video placeholder layer.

In Photoshop, the opaque area of the video placeholder layer determines the size of the video thumbnail back in Encore. If the video placeholder layer is not masked by either a layer mask or a vector mask, then Encore will build the smallest rectangle that will encompass the opaque area, even if the opaque area is not rectangular. The video in the video thumbnail button will appear inside of this rectangle.

If you want the video in a video thumbnail button to appear as a shape other than a rectangle, then you have to use layer and/or vector masks in Photoshop. The mask acts like a shaped window through which the video can be seen. This technique is also a good idea for rectangular video thumbnails, even though Encore defaults to using a rectangular shape for the video placeholder layer. Using a layer/vector mask for rectangular video thumbnails lets you precisely determine what the size of the thumbnail will be in Encore while you are compositing the other button graphics in Photoshop. To create a video placeholder layer in Photoshop:

1   In the Photoshop layers palette, create a new layer set. Give it a name that includes the (+) button prefix.

2   Create a new layer and name it with the (%) video placeholder prefix. If necessary, move the new layer into the new button layer set from Step 1.

3   Draw with the Pen tool or use the Shape tool to create a mask for the new layer. The Toolbar options in use for either the Pen or Shape tool determine whether you need to create a layer mask, create a vector mask, or if drawing the shape automatically masked the layer.

4   If you need to create a vector mask from a path, switch to the Paths palette and choose Layer ▶ Add Vector Mask ▶ Current Path.

5   If you need to create a layer mask from a filled pixel shape, select the new shape and choose Layer ▶ Add Layer Mask ▶ Reveal Selection.

You can create multiple shapes as part of a single vector mask for a layer so that the video will be seen through more than one shape at the same time. This also works for text type that has been converted to a shape, so you can get a video-through-text effect for your thumbnail if you want.

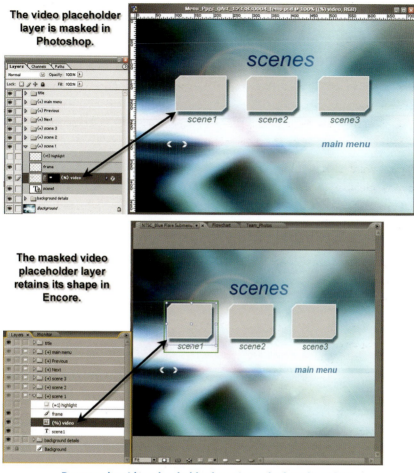

The video placeholder layer is masked in Photoshop.

The masked video placeholder layer retains its shape in Encore.

Because the video placeholder layer is masked in photoshop, it will retain its shape back in Encore

Note: Unlike subpicture highlights, you can add feathered masks and layer effects like bevels and glows to video placeholder layers.

Saving Your Menu

Before saving the menu in Photoshop, there is one more step that you should take if you are not using a CS version of Photoshop. In Photoshop CS, the Standard NTSC DVD image preset size is 720×480 with a pixel aspect ratio (PAR) of 0.9.

The same image preset size in earlier versions of Photoshop, however, is 720×534 with no PAR setting. The difference is that the earlier versions only understand square pixels. This affects what happens to the menu inside of Encore. When a Standard NTSC DVD project is built, Encore will have to scale a 720×534 square-pixel menu to the project dimensions of 720×480 with a PAR of 0.9. But let's consider what happens if you scale the menu in Photoshop, before saving the menu as a .psd file. Theoretically, at least, you should be able to preserve more image quality when compared to having Encore scale the menu. Not only are you scaling a native Photoshop document inside of Photoshop, but you have image-enhancement tools like Unsharp Mask available for use before you save. Encore won't sharpen or otherwise enhance the image when it scales the menu at build time.

To scale a 720×534 square-pixel menu to the Standard NTSC DVD frame size in non-CS versions of Photoshop:

1   Choose Image ▶ Image Size.

2   Near the bottom of the Image Size dialog that appears, uncheck Constrain Proportions.

3   Ensure that Resample Image is checked, and that Bicubic is the current resampling algorithm.

4   In the Height control, change 534 pixels to 480 pixels. Click OK.

5   Touch up the image as necessary to maintain maximum quality.

6   Once the menu is scaled and touched-up, save it as a layered .psd file.

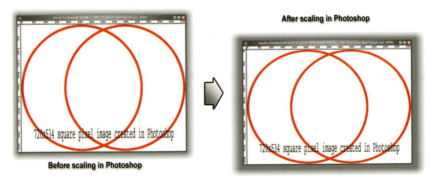

A 720×534 square-pixel image before and after scaling in Photoshop

Note: This scaling of the square-pixel menu will introduce a distortion to all layers of the menu that will be automatically corrected in Encore when the menu is imported and Encore interprets the distorted square pixels as non-square.

Working with Adobe After Effects

The best new feature in Adobe Encore DVD 2.0 that relates to interacting with other Adobe software is the Dynamic Link to Adobe After Effects 7.0. This new feature creates integration between After Effects and Encore that is every bit as powerful and convenient as the link between Encore and Photoshop. When you create a Dynamic Link between an After Effects composition and Encore, a background instance of After Effects without the user interface is started. Inside of Encore, the After Effects composition is "live" – the background instance of After Effects will render the composition as needed when you preview it in Encore. The After Effects composition itself will appear in the Project panel as an asset. You can use the linked After Effects composition just like any other video asset – as a timeline or as a menu background. Once the After Effects composition is added to a timeline or a menu, all of the operations that you would expect are available. You can add chapter markers, set poster frames and add subtitles to a timeline that contains the linked composition, and you can set menu duration, loop point and animate buttons for a menu that contains the composition.

Note: Adobe After Effects thrives on high-speed processors and large amounts of RAM. Experienced users of After Effects will understand why dynamically linking After Effects compositions in Encore is a really good reason to have a computer system that exceeds the recommended system requirements for Adobe Encore DVD 2.0.

To set up a Dynamic Link between Adobe Encore DVD 2.0 and Adobe After Effects 7.0:

1   In Encore, choose File ▶ Adobe Dynamic Link ▶ Import After Effects Composition. Be prepared to wait several seconds while Encore calls up the background After Effects process.

2   In the Import Composition window, navigate in the left pane to the After Effects project that contains the composition to be used for the link.

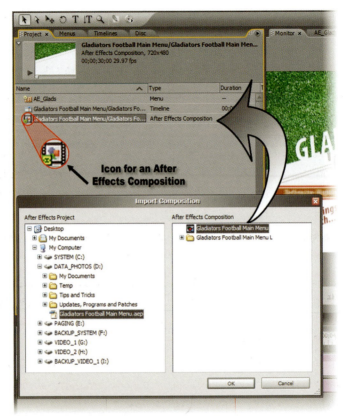

Importing an After Effects composition into Encore

3 In the right pane, navigate to the desired composition and click OK. The selected composition appears in the Encore Project panel as an asset.

If you need to edit the dynamically linked composition back in After Effects, use the Edit ▶ Edit Original (Ctrl+E) command to open the After Effects user interface, where you can make the necessary changes. Since the After Effects composition in Encore is live, when you return to Encore the linked composition will automatically update to reflect the changes you just made in After Effects.

Note: The Dynamic Link feature between Adobe After Effects 7.0 and Adobe Encore DVD 2.0 is only available with the full Adobe Production Studio suite of applications. The individual point products of the suite do not have dynamic linking capability.

Animating an Encore Menu in After Effects

If you don't have the Adobe Production Studio, but you have After Effects version 6.5 or later, you can still take advantage of the integration between After Effects and Encore. You can turn any static menu in Encore into a motion menu by animating its objects in After Effects. Popular design techniques include having buttons and other objects fly in from off-screen and making menu objects fade up in position. If you'd like to turn a static menu into a motion menu by animating its objects in After Effects, here's what you do:

1 Select the Menu you want to animate in the Project panel and choose Menu ▶ Create After Effects Composition.

2 Choose a Save location for the menu in the Save Menu for After Effects dialog so that After Effects knows where to find it. The menu will be saved as a .psd file. After Effects will automatically save the new project to this location as well.

3 When the After Effects user interface opens, the saved menu will appear in the After Effects Project panel as a composition. Buttons and other layer sets appear as nested compositions.

4 Animate the menu objects as desired in After Effects. Don't make button subpicture layers visible in After Effects because they need to stay part of the subpicture overlay back in Encore, and not part of the animated video background.

5 Make sure to leave enough time at the end of the composition, with all objects in their final position, to give the audience plenty of time to make their selection. A minute or more is not unreasonable, even if the menu will loop.

6 Render the composition as a video file from the After Effects Render Queue. Select the Embed Project Link option in the queue so that if you need to edit the animation at a later time you can call up the After Effects project again by using the Edit ▶ Edit Original (Ctrl+E) command in Encore.

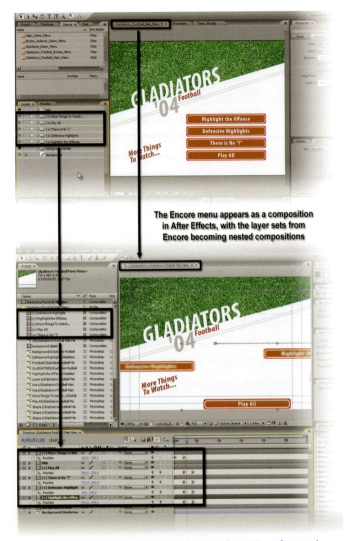

The Encore menu as a composition and a series of nested compositions in After Effects

7 Import the rendered video from After Effects into Encore as an asset. The After Effects video will become the motion background for the menu. Add background audio and set up the menu to loop as desired.

8 Set up highlight-only buttons as discussed in the Advanced Design Techniques section of "The Project: Linking Everything Together".

Working with Adobe Premiere Pro

So far in this book I've talked about using your favorite non-linear editing application, or NLE, to prepare video assets for Encore. Now I get to talk about my favorite NLE, Adobe Premiere Pro. Premiere Pro integrates with Encore in two important areas – chapter marker placement and Edit Original functionality. The latest version of Premiere Pro integrates in the same way as the older versions, but it steals a little bit of Encore's thunder, too. Versions 1.0 and 1.5 of Adobe Premiere Pro included a direct-to-DVD export function that was useful for quick sound and video checks in hardware and software DVD players, but it wasn't very useful for finished discs because there was no menu structure available. In addition, there was no way to save the transcoded files for use or review at a later time. In Premiere Pro 2.0, Adobe has included the ability to add menus to the direct-to-DVD export and to write disc image files that can be accessed at any time. As a further design enhancement, each of Premiere Pro's menu templates can be extensively customized, including motion backgrounds and buttons.

The downside of using Premiere Pro to produce your DVDs is that the menu customization only applies to the current sequence in Premiere Pro; you can't save modified menus as templates like you can in Encore. And many of the advanced design techniques we've discussed are still beyond Premiere Pro's reach. Despite Premiere Pro's improvements to DVD creation, we need to focus on how Premiere Pro can support DVD authoring with Encore.

Placing Chapter Markers for Encore

Sequence markers that you place in a Premiere Pro sequence can become chapter markers in Encore when you add the exported Premiere Pro video asset to a timeline in Encore. Premiere Pro's sequence markers are not automatically exported as chapter markers; you have to set up the sequence markers properly to make that happen. To turn an ordinary sequence marker in Premiere Pro into a bona-fide chapter marker that will appear in Encore:

1 Add unnumbered sequence markers to a Premiere Pro sequence at each point where you would like a chapter marker to appear in Encore. Keep in mind that Encore will automatically add a chapter marker at the beginning of a timeline, but it won't have a name or any comments. If you want to override Encore's generic first chapter marker with a more descriptive one of your own from Premiere Pro, place an unnumbered sequence marker at the beginning of the sequence or work area to be exported.

2 Double-click on each sequence marker in turn and add a name for the chapter in the Chapter field of the Marker Options section of Marker dialog in Premiere Pro. Encore will automatically number the chapters, so it's not very useful to put a chapter number in the Chapter field unless you intend to name your chapters in Encore and just need a placeholder in Premiere Pro.

3 If you wish to add descriptive comments or editorial notes to go along with a marker, add the text to the Comments field at the top of the Marker dialog.

The Marker dialog in Premiere Pro. The Chapter field must be filled in for this marker to be recognized by Encore as a chapter marker

4 If you export the sequence as a Windows .avi file, then the marker comments will only get exported if you select that option from the AVI Compile Options dialog.

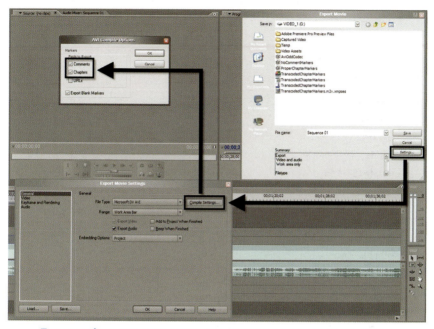

To get marker comments to appear in Encore, the Comments check box in the AVI Compile Options dialog must be selected. The Chapters check box is selected by default

5 If you use the Adobe Media Encoder to export video and audio as elementary MPEG streams, then the chapter names, comments and an embedded project link are included automatically.

6 Export the sequence from Premiere Pro. Make sure to embed a project link when you export so that the Edit Original command in Encore can call up the source project if the asset needs to be edited later.

7 Import the video from Premiere Pro into Encore as a timeline. The sequence markers from Premiere Pro will appear as chapter markers in the new timeline.

The chapter name and comments from Premiere Pro appear in Encore

If you are planning to add multiple video assets to a single timeline in Encore, don't export any chapter marker information from Premiere Pro. Proper support for Premiere Pro chapter markers with multiple assets in a single timeline is not included in this version of Encore. You can do it, but your chapter markers will appear in very strange places inside of Encore.

Note: Adobe Premiere Pro 2.0 introduced a new type of sequence marker – the DVD Marker. Interestingly, DVD Markers in Premiere Pro can't be used as chapter markers in Adobe Encore DVD 2.0. The DVD Markers in Premiere Pro are solely for use with the DVDs that are created by Premiere Pro.

Working with Adobe Audition

Audio is an essential ingredient in any successful video project, and DVD authoring in Encore is no exception. Adobe Audition can create rich, multi-layered session mixes that will really enhance the audio portion of your video assets and slideshows. If you embed a session link in your exported mixdown from Audition, then the Edit Original command in Encore will call up Audition, where you will be given a choice between editing the existing asset in Edit View and modifying the session itself in Multitrack View.

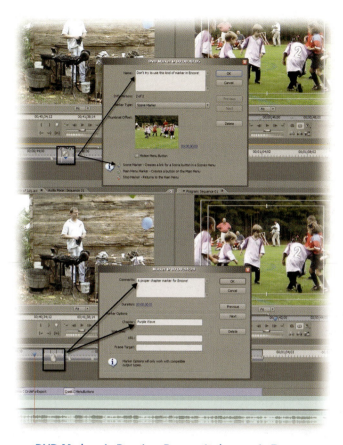

**DVD Markers in Premiere Pro won't show up in Encore.
There is not yet a way to get Encore to recognize the
abundance of information in a Premiere Pro DVD Marker**

Multichannel audio is a hot topic in DVD authoring these days. Almost every
commercial DVD has audio that is encoded as multichannel Dolby Digital or
DTS surround sound, and many authors are seeking ways to include multichannel
audio in their discs. Unfortunately, the tremendous cost involved in licensing a
multichannel Dolby Digital or DTS transcoder has kept that functionality out of
both Adobe Audition and Adobe Encore DVD. Neither application can produce
multichannel audio that is suitable for the DVD-Video format. Audition can produce
multichannel .wav files, but Encore will not import them. Encore will only

The editing choices in Adobe Audition after invoking the Edit Original command from Encore

The audio transcoding setting in Preferences

import multichannel Dolby Digital and DTS audio files. If you need multichannel audio for your finished disc, you will have to transcode your audio in a suitable program and then import it into Encore. The Minnetonka plug-in for Adobe Premiere Pro and Steinberg's Nuendo are examples of applications that can handle multichannel transcoding.

Note: The Dolby Digital transcoder inside of Encore is for two-channel audio only.

Adobe Bridge

New to Encore and the other Adobe Production Studio applications is a feature first introduced in Photoshop CS – Adobe Bridge. Bridge is a file manager with layouts and extra information that are designed specifically for the digital media producer and post-production artist. Adobe Bridge is accessible from inside of Encore via the File ▶ Browse command. It gives the same convenient access to multimedia files from inside of other Adobe applications that Photoshop has had since the introduction of the File Browser palette. Bridge, however, has a much-improved and friendlier interface which increases usability. Think of Bridge as the File Browser palette on "nutritional supplements". The file management functions are much better, and you can assign metadata and searchable keywords to almost any multimedia file. Having this tool at your fingertips inside of Encore can greatly speed up your file management tasks.

Navigation
and File
Management
Toolbar

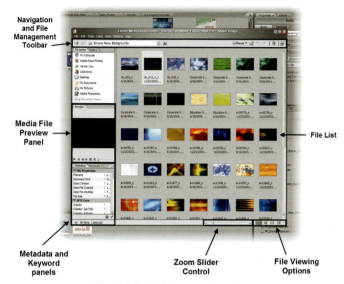

Media File
Preview
Panel

File List

Metadata and
Keyword
panels

Zoom Slider
Control

File Viewing
Options

The Adobe Bridge user interface

Additional Encore DVD Resources

Now that you've had an introduction to authoring DVDs with Adobe Encore DVD 2.0, there are several resources available that can keep you up-to-speed and increase your skills with this powerful application.

I always start with the online help that is available right within Encore whenever I have a question or need some procedural review. You should too. I know that users often get frustrated with the help files for a particular program because it seems they can never find the right information when they need it. The Adobe Help Center's effective search function and detailed table of contents for Encore should help you get the information you need with a minimum amount of hassle.

The Internet has a wealth of information about DVD authoring with Encore. Here are some really good resources that are available on the web:

1   Adobe's User-to-User Forums: http://www.adobe.com/support/forums/ main.html. There is a forum for every Adobe software package, including Encore. These forums are very active, and many of the contributors are knowledgeable and experienced.

2   The Cow: http://forums.creativecow.net/index.html. C-O-W stands for Communities Of the World, and the Creative Cow forums encompass a diverse community of media professionals and enthusiasts. There are articles, tutorials and a free newsletter to enrich you during your visits.

3   Wrigley Video Productions: http://www.wrigleyvideo.com/forum/. Curt Wrigley hosts a forum that has attracted a wide range of users from around the world. Affectionately known as "Wrigleyville", these active forums are a welcoming and friendly place for novice and expert alike. Some of the very best Encore tutorials (free or otherwise) on the net are here at Wrigleyville.

4   DMN Forums: http://www.dmnforums.com/. Digital Media Net hosts a ton of forums and provides a lot of valuable research tools that range from news and reviews to tutorials and career opportunities.

5   Adobe Studio: http://studio.adobe.com/us/search/main.jsp. You'll find more than a few tips and tutorials here to jump start your creative mind as you construct your Encore projects.

Enjoy your journey through the world of DVD authoring with Adobe Encore DVD 2.0! Just remember to brush your teeth and act natural.

Jeff Bellune

Index

Adobe After Effects, 225–227
  Encore menu, animating, 227–229
Adobe Audition, 232–234
Adobe Bridge, 234–235
Adobe Help Center (AHC), 43–44
Adobe Photoshop, 106–107, 140, 142, 143, 214–216
  Edit Menu command, 216–217
  menu, saving, 223–225
  menus, creating, 217–218
  subpicture highlights, 218–221
  video placeholder layers, 221–223
Adobe Premiere Pro, 229
Adobe Production Studio, 16, 214, 226–227
Advanced design techniques, 182–183
After Effects *see* Adobe After Effects
Aliases, 182
Align command, Menu objects, 131–133
Alignment options, 148
Allowable user operations, 180–181
Animate Buttons checkbox, 172–173
Another project element, End Actions, 163
Assets:
  importing, 51–64
  joining, in single timeline, 94–95
  listing, 46
Audio assets, 54, 78, 97
Audio encoding scheme, 13–14
Audio language, 13
Audio Out, 14–15
Audio tracks, adding, 86–87
Audio/Video Out:
  Audio Out, 14–15
  Media Cache Database, 16
  Video Out, 15–16
  Video Playback, 16
Auto Activate, 186
Auto Layout, End Actions, 165–166
Automatic color set, 123–124

Background audio, to menu, 150–152
Background transcoding, 72
Background video, to menu, 153–155

Baseline shift, 147
Bit rate, 14, 69, 74
  Constant Bit Rate, 70
  Variable Bit Rate, 70
Button rollover menus, 186–188
Button routing, 11, 135–138

Cables, 3
CBR, 70
Chapter markers, 82–86
  End Actions, 178–179
  navigation, 86
  placing, 229–232
  poster frames, 83–85
  and transcoded assets, 85
Chapter Playlist, 19, 174–175, 176–177, 178
Character panel, 40, 92, 144, 146–148
  formatting options, 147–148
Check Project, 195, 196, 197, 200
Color, 148
Constant Bit Rate *see* CBR
Current time indicator, 78, 79, 80, 81

Default still length, 11–12
Default subtitle length, 12
Digital video and audio, space requirements, 2
Direct Select tool, 111
Disc panel, 37, 67–68
Distribute command, Menu objects, 133–135
Docking panels, 23, 25–29
  drop zones, 23, 25, 28, 29
Dolby Digital, 13–14, 69, 233
  transcoder, 234
Drop shadow, 146
Drop zones, 23, 25, 28, 29
DTS, 54, 233
Duration control, 151, 153, 184, 190
DV device, 15–16
DVD building:
  Dual-layer discs, 204–206
  DVD disc, 203–204
  DVD folder, 206–208

DVD building (*Continued*)
DVD Image, 208–209
DVD Master, 209–210
DVD-ROM content, 211
preliminary steps, 194–203

Easter Eggs, 121, 185–186
Edit Original command, 214
Encoding:
Audio encoding scheme, 13–14
Maximum Automatic transcoding
bit rate, 14
Encore:
chapter markers, placing,
229–232
DVD resources, additional, 235–236
interaction with other Adobe
software, 213
launching, 6–8
library, 41–42, 47, 55–56, 107, 109–110,
140–142, 155–156, 184, 216
End Actions, 162–165
Another project element, 163
Link Back to Here, 163
Return to Last Menu, 164
Specify Link, 164
Stop, 164
Errors, correcting, 197–199
Extras Menu, 116, 118, 128, 176

Firewire, 3, 15
First Play, 161–162
Floating window, 23, 24, 195
Flowchart, 46–48
Flowchart panel, 38, 39, 159, 160, 162,
164, 165–166, 182
Font:
family list, 147
size, 147
style buttons, 148
style list, 147
see also Character panel
Frames, 18–19
closing, 30
rate, 53
size, 28–29, 52
tabs reordering, 29
wing menu, 23
see also Panels

General, Preferences:
Library Content, 9
Playback Quality, 9
Reset Warning Dialogs, 10
TV Standard, for New Projects, 9
User Interface, 8, 17
Graphic assets, 55

Hardware requirement, 2–3
Highlight Group, 93, 124, 125–127,
128, 188
Horizontal and vertical scales, 147

Import as Asset command, 55–56
Import as Menu command, 60–61
Import as Slideshow command, 57–60
Import as Timeline command, 56–57, 58
Importing assets, 52–64
asset locating, 62–63
asset replacing, 64
asset types, 52–55
import options, 55–61
Info badges, 182
Installation *see* Program loading
Interface:
Adobe Help Center, 43–44
Character panel, 40
Disc panel, 37
Flowchart panel, 38, 39
frames and panels, 18–19
Layers panel, 43
Library panel, 41–42
Menu viewer, 38, 39
Menus panel, 35, 36
Monitor panel, 38
Project panel, 35, 56, 73, 76–77, 101,
152, 163
Properties panel, 40
Slideshow viewer, 41
Styles panel, 42–43
Timeline viewer, 40–41
Timelines panel, 35, 36
toolbar, 34
viewers, 19
workspaces, 19–22, 34
workspaces, arranging, 22–32
workspaces, customizing, 32–33

Kerning, 147

Layers panel, 43, 112, 113, 116, 118, 119, 120, 142
Leading, 147
Library, 47, 55–56, 107, 109–110, 155–156, 184, 216
 Library Content, 9
 Library panel, 41–42
 usage, 140–142
Link Back to Here, End Actions, 163, 168
Linking:
 advanced design techniques, 182–183
 Auto Layout, 165–166
 button highlights, 183–185
 button rollover menus, 186–188
 chapter marker End Action, 178–179
 Easter Eggs, 185–186
 End Actions, 162–165
 First Play, 161–162
 Flowchart Panel, 182
 Menu buttons, 166–168
 Navigation Design workspace, 159–161
 overrides, 180
 Playlists, 174–178
 remote buttons, 173–174
 Sync Button Text and Name, 168–169
 Trivia Quiz games, 188–192
 user operations, 180–181
 video thumbnail buttons, 170–173

Main Menu, 116, 117, 118, 187
Maximum Automatic transcoding bit rate, 14
Media Cache Database, 16
Menu buttons, 119, 130, 173
 creation, 142–143
 links, 166–168
 routing, 135–138
Menu Color Set, 123–127
 Automatic color set, 123–124
 dialog, 124, 126–127
 Menu Default color set, 123, 124
Menu objects:
 aligning and distributing, 130–135
 Direct Select tool, 111
 duplicating, 116–117
 menu button, 119
 Move tool, 111, 113
 Selection tool, 111

 style effects, adding, 149–150
 text, replacing, 114–115
Menu Remote link, 174
Menu viewer, 19, 20, 38, 39, 41, 110, 111, 122, 144
Menus panel, 35, 36
Menus, 10–11
 animating, in After Effects, 227–229
 background audio, 150–152
 background video, 153–155
 building from scratch, 138
 button routing, 135–138
 buttons, creating, 142–143
 Character panel, 146–148
 creation, external to Encore, 143–144
 creation, for project, 107–110
 creation, from backgrounds, 140
 duplication, 115–116
 Library, 140–142
 Main Menu, 116, 117, 118, 187
 Menu Color Set, 123–127
 Menu Design workspace, 107, 108
 Menu viewer, 38, 39
 Menus panel, 35, 36
 Motion menu, 153–155, 156
 objects see Menu objects
 as Photoshop files, 106–107
 safe area, 113–114
 saving, in Photoshop, 223–225
 saving, to Library, 155–156
 static menu backgrounds, 139–140
 styles, 149–150
 subpicture highlight, 120–123, 127–130
 text object to button, conversion, 118–120
 text object, adding, 144–146
 text objects, resizing, 148–149
 wing menu, 23
Monitor panel, 38, 80–81, 88
 display quality, 81
Motion menu, 153–155, 156
Move tool, 111, 113
Multichannel audio, 233–234

Navigation Design workspace, 159–161
Non-linear editor (NLE), 73, 94, 95, 183–184
 Adobe Premiere Pro, 229
NTSC, 3, 7, 53, 139, 223, 224

One-pass transcoding, 70
Orphan elements, 38
Overrides, 180

PAL, 3, 7, 53
Panels, 18–19
    Character panel, 40, 92, 144,
        146–148
    closing, 30
    Disc panel, 37, 67–68
    docking, 23, 25–29
    Flowchart panel, 38, 39, 159, 160, 164,
        165–166, 182
    interface, 8, 18
    Layers panel, 43, 112, 113, 116, 118,
        119, 120, 142
    Library panel, 41–42
    Menus panel, 35, 36
    Monitor panel, 38, 80–81, 88
    opening, 31–32
    Project panel, 35, 56
    Properties panel, 38, 40, 94, 98, 102, 136,
        152, 161, 164, 167–168, 172, 175
    Styles panel, 42–43
    Timelines panel, 35, 36
    undocking, 30
    viewers, 19
    see also Frames
PAR, 53, 95, 99, 139
Photoshop see Adobe Photoshop
Pixel aspect ratio see PAR
Planning, for project:
    flowchart, 46–48
    listing assets, 46
    workflow, 48–49
Playback, 13, 16, 173
    Monitor panel, 38, 80
    Playback Quality, 9, 81
Player region code, 13
Playlists, 174–178
Poster frames, 83–85
Preferences setup:
    Audio/Video Out, 14–16
    Encoding, 13–14
    Encore, launching, 6–8
    General, 8–10
    Menus, 10–11
    Preview, 12–13
    Timelines, 11–12

Premiere Pro see Adobe Premiere Pro
Preview:
    Audio language, 13
    Player region code, 13
    Subtitle language, 13
    TV mode, 12–13
Program loading, 3–4
    hardware requirement, 2–3
Project flowchart, 108, 158–159
Project panel, 35, 56, 73, 76–77, 101,
    152, 163
    after importing assets, 61–62
Properties panel, 38, 40, 94, 98, 102, 136,
    152, 161, 164, 167–168, 172, 175

Remote buttons, 173–174
Reset Warning Dialogs, 10
Resume, End Actions, 168
Return to Last Menu, End Actions, 164

Safe Area, 113–114
    Action Safe Area, 113
    Title Safe Area, 113, 114
Scaling images, 97–98
Selection tool, 111
Slideshow, 76, 175, 177, 208, 232
    creation, 99
    effects and transitions, adding, 101–102
    Import as Slideshow command, 57–60
    scaling images, 97–98
    slides, arranging, 100–101
    Slideshow Design workspace, 95–96
    Slideshow Viewer, 19, 38, 41, 97
    still images and audio, adding, 96–97
    subtitles, adding, 102–104
    widescreen Slideshows, 98–99
Specify Link, End Actions, 164, 168
Static menu backgrounds, 139–140
Still images and audio, adding to
    Slideshow, 96–97
Stop, End Actions, 164, 168
Style effects, adding to menu objects,
    149–150
Styles panel, 42–43
Subpicture highlight, 120–123
    additional colors, 218–221
    appearance, changing, 127–128
    special effect, 128–130
    three states, 122

Subtitles:
  adding, 87–91, 102–104
  language, 13
  Monitor panel, 88–89
  to slideshow, 102–104
  Subtitle Workshop, importing, 91
  text appearance, changing, 91–93
Sync button Text and Name, 168–169

Text Antialias Mode, 148
Text object to button, conversion, 118–120
Text objects:
  adding, to menu, 144–146
  resizing, 148–149
Time ruler, 78
Timeline Color Set, 92, 92–93
Timeline creation, 75, 76–78
  assets, joining, 94–95
  audio tracks adding, 86–87
  chapter marker, 82–86
  Monitor panel, 80–81
  navigation, 78–80, 86
  Poster frame setting, 83–85
  slideshow, 95–104
  subtitle text, 91–93
  subtitles, adding, 87–91
  Timeline Editing workspace, 76
  Timeline Viewer, 78–80
  Timelines panel, 35, 36
Timelines, 175, 177, 178, 181
  Color Set, 92, 92–93
  creation see Timeline creation
  Default still length, 11–12
  Default subtitle length, 12
  Editing, 76
  Import as Timeline command, 56–57, 58
  Timeline panel, 35, 36
  Timeline Viewer, 19, 20, 38, 40–41,
    78–80, 179
Title button, 173–174
Title Safe Area, 89, 91, 103, 113, 114,
  131–132, 133, 134, 135
Toolbar, 34
Tracking, 147

Transcoding, 65–74
  automatic setting, 67
  before import, 73–74
  DVD-5, 67, 69, 70, 74
  presets, 71–72
  settings, 68–72
  within Encore, 72–73
Trivia Quiz games, 188–192
TV mode, 12–13
TV Standard, 9
Two-pass transcoding, 70, 72
Type icons, 182

User Interface see Interface

Variable Bit Rate (VBR), 70, 70–71, 72
Video assets, 52–53, 69, 71, 77–78, 153,
  155, 232
Video Out, 15–16
Video placeholder layers, 221–223
Video Playback, 16
Video thumbnail buttons, 170–173
  Animate Buttons checkbox, 172–173
  special properties, 171
Viewers, 19
  closing, 31
  Menu viewer, 19, 20, 38, 39, 41, 110,
    111, 122, 144
  opening, 31–32
  Slideshow viewer, 19, 38, 41, 97
  Timeline Viewer, 19, 20, 38, 40–41,
    78–80, 179

Widescreen Slideshows, 98–99
Wing menu, 23
Workspaces, 19–22, 34
  arrangement, 22–32
  customization, 32–33
  Menu Design, 107
  Navigation Design, 159–161
  resetting, 32
  Slideshow Design, 95–96
  Timeline Editing, 76
Wrapping, 11

Zoom slider, 78–79, 97